THE HOLY LAND

How to use this book

The main text provides a survey of the country's cultural history from the Early Bronze Age to the present day. It is illustrated with general views, archaeological sites, sculpture and painting.

A map of the Holy Land (p. 256) shows the principal archaeological sites, cities and historic monuments.

To find a museum or gallery turn to Appendix I, which lists them alphabetically by towns, with their addresses, opening times and a note on their scope and contents.

To find an archaeological site or a city turn to Appendix II. Under the entries for the large cities are listed alphabetically the main places of interest therein. Grid-references enable the most important places to be easily located on the map (e. g. Jerusalem, GC, means horizontal reference G, vertical reference C). All places are cross-referenced in the index and there is a glossary of archaeological terms.

For information on artists - architects, painters and sculptors, mainly of the 20th century, whose buildings and works of art are to be seen there - turn to Appendix III.

World Cultural Guides

THE HOLY LAND

Michael Avi-Yonah

169 illustrations
in colour and black and white

special photography
by Mario Carrieri

Thames and Hudson · London

The LORD is the God of the whole earth,
the mountains of Judah belong to him,
to the God of Jerusalem.
The Mount of Moriah Thou hast favoured,
LORD.

Inscription in a burial cave near Amaziah, about 700 BC

Chapter XVIII translated from the French by Suzanne Sale.

The World Cultural Guides
have been devised and produced by
Park and Roche Establishment, Schaan.

French edition by Editions Albin Michel, Paris.

ISBN 0 500 64008 4

Printed in Italy by Amilcare Pizzi S.p.A.

Contents

Jacket: Kefar Bar'am Synagogue

End-paper: Ancient Jerusalem as
imagined by an anonymous
nineteenth-century Russian painter

Significant dates
in the history of the Holy Land

BC

3150-1200	Early, Middle and Late Bronze Ages, Canaan inhabited by the Amorites, Hurrites, Hittites, etc.
1290-1224	Reign of Rameses II marks decline in Egyptian power. Israelite conquest of Canaan.
1200-1020	Period of the Judges. Introduction of iron into general use, associated with Philistine invasion and settlement in the coastal plain.
1020-1004	Reign of Saul. Israel united in one kingdom.
1004-965	Reign of David. Jerusalem established as national and religious centre.
965-928	Reign of Solomon. Trade routes to Mesopotamia, Asia Minor, Arabia and Africa established. Palace and first Temple in Jerusalem built.
928	Division of kingdom into Israel and Judah.
882-842	Dynasty of Omri in Israel. The first prophets, Elijah and Elisha.
853	Ahab, king of Israel, and his allies defeat the Assyrians at Qarqar.
733-586	The great prophets in Jerusalem: Isaiah, Jeremiah, Ezekiel.
723	Fall of Samaria to the Assyrians. End of Kingdom of Israel.
586	Jerusalem falls to Nebuchadnezzar. Exile of Jews to Babylon.
537	Persian conquest of Babylon and return of Jews from exile.
519	Dedication of second Temple in Jerusalem.
332	Alexander the Great defeats the Persians.
301	Ptolemaic rule begins. Strong Hellenistic influence in Judaea.
200	Power passes to the Seleucids with Antiochus III.
164	Hasmonaean revolt against religious oppression of Antiochus IV.
141-63	Independent Hasmonaean state.
63	Jerusalem captured by Roman general Pompey.
40	Herod appointed in Rome as king of the Jews.
37-4	Herod rules Jerusalem and rebuilds Temple.
5	Birth of Christ.
AD 26-36	Pontius Pilate, procurator of Judaea.
30?	Crucifixion of Christ.

41-44	Reign of Agrippa I, grandson of Herod.
66	Great Revolt against the Romans.
70	Siege of Jerusalem and destruction of Temple.
74	Fall of Masada. Revolt finally crushed.
132-35	Second Revolt led by Simeon Bar Kosiba (Bar Kokhba).
135	Hadrian orders the expulsion of the "circumcised" from Aelia Capitolina (Jerusalem). Judaea renamed Syria-Palaestina.
135-324	Jews confined peacefully to Galilea. Beginning of Talmudic era.
324	Constantine, the first Christian emperor, occupies Palestine.
326	Constantine and his mother, Helena, begin transformation of Jerusalem into a Christian city.
527-65	Reign of Justinian I.
614	Persian invasion of Palestine, with help of a Jewish retreat.
630	Muslim invasion from Arabia.
638	Jerusalem falls to the Muslims.
661	Establishment of Umayyad caliphate.
691	Dome of the Rock built by Abd el-Malik.
750	Abbasid dynasty. Decline of Arab rule.
1096-99	First Crusade begun as joint French-Norman expedition.
1099	Crusader capture of Jerusalem. Establishment of Latin Kingdom.
1187	Saladin captures Jerusalem.
1189	Crusader rule re-established at Acre and along the coast.
1291	Fall of Acre and end of Crusader Kingdom.
1291-1516	Rule of the Mamelukes.
1516	Holy Land falls to the Turks and becomes part of the Ottoman Empire.
1543	Suleiman I (the Magnificent) rebuilds the walls of Jerusalem.
1917	Balfour Declaration that British government favours the "establishment in Palestine of a national home for the Jewish people".
1918-48	Period of British Mandate.
1948	Proclamation of State of Israel.

Prehistory

Cultural life in the Holy Land might be said to have begun about a million years ago with the appearance of the first human beings in this area. The main geographical features of the country, as we know them at present, were already there: its position as a land bridge between Asia and Africa, and between the Mediterranean and the Red Sea; its division into a coastal plain, a central mountain belt and a rift valley.

If the general configuration of the country in prehistoric times could still be recognized by a visitor today, this could not be said of its climate. In prehistoric times torrential rains, combined with a warm climate, resulted in an exuberant forest vegetation. Among the finds from this period are tusks of elephants, teeth and bones of the hippopotamus and the rhinoceros, victims of the hunting skill of early man. Nomads from Africa took advantage of the land bridge between Africa and Asia and settled near the Sea of Galilee, where they found ample sustenance. The earliest settlers were mainly food-gatherers and occasional hunters. Their great resource was their capacity for making tools.

In the first stage, prehistoric man used pebbles to which he gave a rough cutting edge. This first 'pebble culture' was replaced in due course by the 'hand-axe' or 'biface' culture. The hand-axe with its serrated edge and pear-shaped form fitted the hand better. It was the typical tool of the Lower or Earlier Old Stone Age (the Palaeolithic Age), which lasted from about 300,000 BC to some 70,000 years ago.

Even in the Lower Palaeolithic Age, however, the primitive hand-axe was being replaced by flints with triangular pointed tips designed as spears and daggers.

A significant change in climate occurred in the Upper (Later) Palaeolithic Age (up to 14,000 BC). The wet era came to an end, the forests disappeared, and with them went the sub-tropical fauna. The population now split into two groups, one living on the coastal and river lands, which still retained much of their fertility, the other roaming over the slowly desiccating highlands.

Palaeanthropus palaestinus belonged to a variant of the Neanderthal strain of early man. This was a fairly well-developed race with elongated skulls, thick bones above the eyebrows and a wide nose. They were strong, and showed the first glimmerings of spiritual life.

◁
The Sea of Galilee around which much of the story of the Gospels occurred, according to Christian tradition.

Their dead were buried and the graves surrounded by a ring of stones. Objects of daily use and hand-made decoration were added.

In the Mesolithic (Middle Stone) Age (about 14,000 to 7,000 BC) there were social and cultural developments. In the coastal area a mixed economy of food gathering and hunting developed. The inventions of the bow and the trap fall into this period: the hunters were now accompanied by dogs. The first works of art (statuettes of men and beasts, tools fashioned in the resemblance of animals) began to be shaped. Privileged people were buried more elaborately than common mortals. Houses were built of stone. There is also some evidence of trade: sea-shells and dentalia have been found near inland caves.

In the third Stone Age culture, the Neolithic or New Stone Age, the human remains are of full-grown *Homo sapiens*. Economy is based on hoe-agriculture, at least in the Jordan Valley (the Yarmukian culture near Shaar ha-Golan and the Jericho oasis), and is associated with a fertility cult. The figurines found at Shaar ha-Golan, with their stress on primary and secondary genital organs, are clear evidence of this. Another important development was that in favourable circumstances agriculture began to leave a surplus, which made possible the maintenance of a more leisured social class.

About 7000 BC a Neolithic settlement arose at Jericho (Tell Abu Sultan), which was the first fortified city in the Holy Land. It had a wall, a moat and a round tower with an internal staircase. Visitors to the Neolithic remains of Jericho may wonder about material evidence for the story in *Joshua* 6 concerning the miraculous capture of Jericho after the collapse of its walls, following a trumpet blast. For confirmation one would have to find Late Bronze Age walls around the city but Jericho of the Canaanite period had walls of the Early Bronze Age built upon Neolithic remains. These were surrounded by a glacis with a supporting wall of the Middle Bronze Age. The settlement was destroyed about 1560 BC. Jericho was resettled between 1400 and the end of the fourteenth century, but the town was poor and the earlier walls were re-used. There is no evidence of a violent destruction after the end of the Middle Bronze Age.

The religious needs of Neolithic Jericho were provided for by a temple in which a trinity of gods (male, female and child) was worshipped. The belief in survival after death was expressed in the practice of covering the skulls of the dead with plaster to create a lifelike effect.

The earliest pottery was sun-dried, but, as it remained porous, firing in kilns was later introduced. The making of pottery involved two technical processes of great future importance: the careful regulation of fire for the kilns, by which man learned to control this element for his purposes; and the transformation of natural clay into a man-made material of different quality, namely pottery.

The last prehistoric period was the Chalcolithic Age (4000-3150 BC). The typical cultures of this period were discovered in the Jordan Valley (Jericho and Tuleilat Ghassul east of the river), in the coastal plain (Azor, near Tel Aviv), and in the Negev (Beer Matar and Beer Safad near Beersheba, Engeddi and the caves of the Judaean desert).

As the name of the period indicates (Chalcolithic from Greek *chalkos*, 'copper' and *lithos*, 'stone') metal objects of cast copper first appear in this age. The copper was obtained from the mines of the Arava (the rift valley between the Dead Sea and Elath) or from further afield. It was heated in clay ovens and cast in moulds.

A Chalcolithic sanctuary has been discovered at Engeddi; it consists of a sacred enclosure (*temenos*) which is entered through an elaborate gateway with a waiting room, and a simpler side-door. In one corner of the enclosure is a single room (a store-room or dwelling for the priest or priests). The holy of holies is an oblong room (2 by 5 m.) with an entrance in one long side and the altar, shaped like a horseshoe around a calcite base, opposite. Benches run along the long sides of the room. On both sides of the altar are depressions in the ground, used for remnants of offerings. A circular 'altar' stands in the middle of the room, with a drainage channel leading from it.

Other remnants of the Chalcolithic religion are the ivory figurines from Beersheba. One is the figurine of a nude man with arms crossed. The eyes, hair and beard were once added with some material other than ivory. Another figurine, with its head missing, represents a pregnant woman in the same posture. A third is the upper part of a female, a fourth a bird, a fifth a bell-shaped object.

A third manifestation of Chalcolithic religiosity is found in the os-suaries located in tombs in the coastal plain. These are pottery boxes, 30-70 cm. in length, representing miniature models of houses. The cover is the roof, domed or gabled; the body of the house stands on pillars, a necessity in the swampy soil of the coastal area; an opening (which sometimes even has on its side protrusions imitating locks) represents the door. Some of these 'homes' are provided with

The Dead Sea into whose waters the River Jordan runs. 1300 feet below sea level, the water is intensely saline.

Clay ossuaries. Bone containers in the form of houses for secondary burial from Azor excavations. Chalcolithic Period. Israel Museum.

ornaments (painted or in relief) which suggest the features of men. A curved nose projects from some, while others have painted eyes.

In 1961 one of the caves in the Hever Valley (now appropriately named 'Cave of the Treasure') yielded a cache of over 450 objects, mostly of finely-cast copper, but a few in haematite or ivory. The objects include some tools and weapons, but seem to have had in the main a ritual purpose. Some of them are 'crowns', heavy metal circles decorated in shapes like temple gates, with birds perched on them; others seem to be magic wands or sceptres with heads of ibexes or birds of prey. The whole appears to have constituted the treasure of a temple—a very rich one by standards of the time.

Canaan

The Canaanite period in the history of the Holy Land (or the Early, Middle and Later Bronze Ages) lasted from about 3150 to 1200 BC. With it the country entered the age of history. Owing to contacts with the outside world, where writing had already been developed in the fourth millennium, if not earlier, and to the creation of powerful empires in the Nile and Euphrates-Tigris Valleys, Canaan and its inhabitants acquired a definite historical character. It was then inhabited by a branch of the Semitic family of nations, called Amorites ('People

of the West'). One section of this group were the Kinaahu ('People of the Purple', an allusion to the purple dye produced on the coasts of Phoenicia) or Canaanites. This name, originally applied to the Phoenicians only, was gradually extended to all inhabitants of the Holy Land before the coming of the Israelites.

Bronze Age culture was based on the material achievements of the Neolithic and Chalcolithic Ages, but was predominantly urban in character. Most of the historical cities of the Holy Land, Hazor in the north, Megiddo and Beth Shean in the Jezreel valley, Shechem Gezer, Jerusalem and Hebron in the central mountains, became walled cities in the Early Bronze period.

Canaan was split up into a number of city-states, each in theory the possession of its god or *baal*, and each ruled on behalf of the god by a priest-king or by a group of leaders.

The great power centres of the Orient, the Nile Valley and the Mesopotamian plain, began to show their strength in the Early Bronze period. Egypt, the nearest to Canaan, was also the first to emerge. The hieroglyph of Narmer, a Pharaoh of the First Dynasty, appears on a sherd found at Tell Erani ('Areini') in the south. Sneferu of the Fourth Dynasty sent ships along the coast, and Pepi of the Sixth Dynasty reached the promontory of the 'Gazelle's Head' or Mount Carmel.

During the Sixth, Twelfth, Eighteenth and Nineteenth Dynasties,

Egypt advanced into Canaan and Syria. In some cities Egyptian governors were appointed, in others the local kings became vassals of the Pharaoh. Garrisons were left at strategic points, such as Beth Shean. The decline of the Old Kingdom in the last quarter of the third millennium led to a state of anarchy. Many of the Canaanite cities were destroyed and abandoned, while a nomad population spread far and wide over Canaan and the northern Negev.

Egyptian power revived after an 'Intermediate Period' in the Middle Bronze Age II (2000-1750 BC), when the Pharaohs of the Twelfth Dynasty extended their sway. One of them, Senusert III (1878-1843 BC), reached the city of Shechem. The invading Hyksos (the 'Shepherd Kings'), a coalition of Semitic tribes with Indo-Aryan allies, expelled the Egyptians and founded an Asian-African empire with its capital in the Lower Delta. The Hyksos were expelled in their turn in the sixteenth century BC by the Pharaohs of the New Kingdom. Pharaoh

Fragments of ivory inlay from a wooden box found in the palace of the ancient Egyptian residence at Tell Fara. Rockefeller Museum.

Thutmosis III (1501-1447 BC) reached the Euphrates. In the second half of the eighteenth century BC Egyptian power diminished, in the interval between the Eighteenth and Nineteenth Dynasties. It revived under the Pharaohs of the Nineteenth Dynasty, especially under Rameses II (1292-1225 BC). His name is engraved on bronze gates found in the excavations of the ancient mound of Jaffa. Egyptian governors ruled over Canaanite cities from Gaza to Beth Shean. One of them is depicted on a box of burnt ivory, together with his suite; he is represented as feasting in the presence of dancing girls. At Beth Shean a statue of Rameses III, a stele of Seti I describing his victories over the nomads of Galilee, and a scarab, showing Rameses II shooting his bow, were found. All these are now at the Rockefeller Museum in Jerusalem.

Even at the height of its greatness, Egypt faced strong cultural competition from Mesopotamia. Fragments of the Babylonian Gilgamesh epic have been discovered at Megiddo, and pottery models of livers, used for teaching divination by the Babylonian method of hepatoscopy, at both Megiddo and Hazor (all these objects are now in the Israel Museum).

The Bronze Age cities of Canaan were founded on small natural elevations which had been chosen for earlier settlements in the Chalcolithic period. After surrounding themselves with strong walls in the Early

Bronze Age and suffering destruction in the Intermediate Bronze Age, the bigger and more prosperous cities of the Middle Bronze Age were built on the ruins of their predecessors. This process was repeated again and again; and the natural mound, topped by the debris of period after period, rose higher and higher over its surroundings. No wonder that the Israelite spies were frightened of the 'very great and walled cities' of Canaan (*Numbers 13:28*) and that Moses ordered his people to go in against 'cities great and fortified up to heaven' (*Deut. 9:1*).

Because of their great antiquity and their rough construction of uncut stones, the remains of the Canaanite cities have for the most part disappeared. The places mentioned below are still visible to the ordinary tourist who does not wish to go out of his way and visit the less accessible sites.

In Jerusalem the Jebusite wall, which ringed the city before the conquest of David, can be seen near the Gihon Source in the eastern slope

of the 'Ophel'. It belonged originally to the Middle Bronze Age (about 1800 BC) and is built of rough boulders. The width of the wall is 2.5 m.

At Beth Yerah, near the Sea of Galilee, an Early Bronze silo has been uncovered. It consists of a wall 10 m. wide, which enclosed three sides of a court; the whole structure measures 40 by 30 m. It is built of rough stones, with a street around it. On top of the wall are sunk circles 10 cm. deep, with foundations of cross walls. These circles were probably the bases of the store houses in which the surplus grain of the Canaanite city was kept. The structure, which consists of over a million stones, shows the social cohesion and the availability of labour in Bronze Age cities.

At Megiddo most of the visible remains belong to the Israelite period. The Early Bronze Age wall at Megiddo has, however, been preserved to a height of 4 m.; its total width is 8 m. It was built in sections, which are still traceable. Three Early Bronze Age temples have also been preserved at Megiddo; they are built on the same plan: a porch in front, with protruding side-walls and two columns in the entrance, and a sanctuary, with a podium for the statue of the god in its back wall; the sanctuary roof was also supported by two columns. There is also an open-air 'high place' or *bamah*, a circular structure built of stone, with a staircase leading to its top.

A similar temple, with a row of columns and a 'high place' adjoining it in an open court, is visible at Nahariya near the seashore. The temple dates from the Middle Bronze period; it shows the same tripartite division (porch, sanctuary and holy of holies—a scheme followed by Solomon in his temple, cf. *1 Kings 6*).

The Bronze Age city of Hazor is the largest of those preserved, as befits a city which was 'the head of all those kingdoms' (of Northern Canaan) (*Joshua 11:10*). Besides the usual high mound there is a huge lower city, 1000 by 700 m. It was defended by a glacis of *terre pisée*. One of the gates has been preserved; there were originally three gateways between pilasters, with two inner courts separating one gate from the other. Another piece of Bronze Age walling at Hazor was found in the north-eastern corner of the acropolis: a corner tower with rounded edges, built of rough stones; it sloped down to form a glacis. In front of it was a narrow fosse, with a counterscarp. The lower city contained a temple complex, also built on the tripartite plan, at least in the last stages (fourteenth century BC). It had a vestibule, a sanctuary and a holy of holies, with a niche in the back wall for the statue of the god. The walls of all three rooms are lined with basalt blocks. In the entrance these have the form of orthostats shaped like lions. A palace with two courts and an elaborate system of water conduits also stands in the lower city. The remains of Hazor bear witness to the high standard of Canaanite architecture and of its relationship to those of the other countries of the ancient Orient, in particular Syria and Asia Minor.

One development in Canaan which was of world importance was the evolution of the alphabetic script in the Middle Bronze Age. The two methods of writing used until then were the cuneiform (syllabic) script of Mesopotamia and the hieroglyphs of Egypt. The former was adapted to the alphabet in Ugarit (Syrian coast), but the adaptation of the hieroglyphs, first discovered in the Sinai (and hence called the proto-Sinaitic), proved more practical. One of the earliest signs of alphabetic writing appears on a sherd found at Gezer. It is incised with three characters: an open hand (*kaf* in Hebrew), a tongue (*lashon*), and a schematic plan of a house (*bayit*) the three signs together forming the biblical name Caleb (KLB in the consonantic Semitic writing). There is a direct link between this script and the Phoenician and Hebrew alphabets, which in turn lead on to the Greek and Latin script of today.

The Middle Bronze Age is also the age of the Patriarchs. Abraham and his descendants followed their flocks in the semi-desert, half-sown areas which were not yet densely settled, occasionally staying for some time near a friendly city, as Shechem for example, sometimes engaging in well-digging and reclaiming a promising piece of land, which happened near Gerar, Beersheba and Rehoboth on the fringes of the Negev desert. The early Canaanite sanctuaries, especially the open-air ones such as that of Nahariya, give us an idea of the places of worship set up at Bethel or Hebron, at which Abraham worshipped.

The only monuments which the wandering patriarchs had of necessity to leave *in situ* were their burial places. Tradition has it that Abraham bought for this purpose the cave of Machpelah near Hebron from

▷

A view to the southeast from the walls of the Old City of Jerusalem across David's City (Ophel) towards the Mount of Evil Counsel.

Pottery vase in the form of a bearded human head, ornamented with punctured decoration, in the style of the so-called Yehudiye vases from Jericho. Middle Bronze Age. Rockefeller Museum.

Ephron the Hittite for four hundred shekels of silver (*Genesis 23*). The location of this cave in what is now the Hebron Haram goes at least as far back as the period of the Second Temple; for it was then that King Herod surrounded the site with a high wall. The cave of Machpelah has kept its secrets; since the time of the Crusaders no one seems to have entered the rock-cut caves (if they exist) under the structure now visible. What can be seen is a Crusader church with pointed arches built within the Herodian enclosure; later it was transformed into a mosque. The cenotaphs within are Mameluke constructions of the fourteenth century; the assignment of each of these structures to a patriarch or one of their wives in based on tradition only.

Historians have also been busy with the determination of the site of the Oaks of Mamre, where Abraham dwelt in the vicinity of Hebron (*Gen. 13:18*) and where the Lord appeared to him (*Gen. 18:1*). In the Herodian period, at a time when the traditional site of the Machpelah cave was walled in, another enclosure was erected around the 'well of Abraham' at a site known today as er-Ramet el-Khalil, 3 km. north of Hebron. It remained a place of worship in Byzantine times, where Christians, Jews and pagans prayed together even after the Emperor Constantine had erected a church in the eastern half of the enclosure. In later times another site, nearer the town of Hebron on its western side, was identified with the 'Oaks of Mamre'—probably because of the very old tree standing there.

Cultic pottery mask found at Hazor in a pottery workshop near small temple with the statue. Middle Bronze Age. Israel Museum.

The descent into Egypt might be historically connected with the Hyksos invasion of *c.* 1750 BC. Among the Hyksos rulers in Egypt there appear Semitic names, such as Yaqub-El, which strongly recall Hebrew names. The change in the relationship between the Egyptians and the Hebrews might be connected with the expulsion of the Hyksos kings and the establishment of the New Kingdom of Egypt.

Another problem is the relationship of the Hebrews with the Hapiru or Habiru, a group of people frequently mentioned in Egyptian and cuneiform texts. These were tribes of wanderers, moving on the fringes of settled society and serving the mercenaries and occasionally the thieves of contemporary Canaan. The root of their name (*apr* means 'dusty') implied that the wanderers were people with dusty feet. The Hapiru are known throughout the ancient Orient, in the western half of the 'Fertile Crescent' from the Euphrates to the Egyptian border. They seem to have been opponents of Egyptian domination, allying themselves with those minor Canaanite kings who rebelled against the Pharaoh. The Israelite tribes seem to have been a subsection of this group.

The long reign of Rameses II (1292-1225 BC) marks the beginning of

P. 19/20
Aerial view of Hebron.

the decline of Egyptian power. For all his grandiloquence, Rameses was forced to negotiate with the Hittites on an equal footing after the drawn battle of Kadesh (1286 BC). The Egyptian hold on Canaan was growing weaker. The later Pharaohs still held the main international roads crossing Canaan, and had garrisons in fortresses such as Gaza and Beth Shean.

The biblical account gives a simplified version of the campaign of Joshua, describing the conquest of Canaan as a single event. Literary sources and archaeological evidence suggest that it was a long drawn-out struggle. One Israelite group settled in the wooded hills of Galilee, leaving aside the fertile plains in which the Canaanite cities stood. Other groups seem to have come from the south. One main body was that attributed to Joshua and his campaign; there is evidence of widespread destruction by fire of the Canaanite cities of the Judaean mountains, from Bethel (in the neighbourhood of Ai) to Lachish. Hazor, the great city of the northern Jordan Valley, also feel and was destroyed about the middle of the thirteenth century BC, the presumed time of the Israelite conquest. On the famous stele of Merneptah, the successor of Rameses II on the throne of Egypt, there occurs the first mention of the name Israel among the cities and peoples of Canaan: 'Israel is laid waste, his seed is not'. Thus in the year 1220 BC the long-living nation first appears on the historical stage.

Pottery incens
stand from
Ashdod.
Philistine,
Iron Age.

Ancient Israel

The Israelite or Iron Age period lasted from the twelfth century BC to the destruction of Jerusalem by Nebuchadnezzar in 586 BC. During this period the Holy Land emerges into the full light of history, both because there now exist relatively numerous written sources, first and foremost the Bible: *Joshua, Judges*, the Books of *Samuel* and of *Kings*, the *Chronicles*; and also because of the archaeological evidence in this and the other countries of the ancient Orient. Historically, the Israelite period can be divided into three stages: the period of settlement (the Judges, 1200-1020 BC), that of the united monarchy, Saul, David and Solomon, and that of the divided monarchy, from Rehoboam to Zedekiah.

During the first of these stages an important event occurred in the history of culture, namely the introduction of iron into general use. Its appearance in this country was connected with the Philistines who were invaders from overseas. For a century and a half they struggled with Israel for the possession of Canaan, until subdued by David.

The period of the Judges (military leaders and impermanent) was one of sharp decline in material standards. The houses built by the victorious Israelites on the ruins of the conquered Canaanite cities were poorer in material and equipment than those they superseded; the Israelite pottery of Iron Age I also marks a decline in standards of technique, ornament and decoration.

Quite possibly this decline indicates not only the cultural gap between the rude conquerors from the desert and the sophisticated city people: it may also reflect the fact that throughout the period of the Judges, the Israelite tribes were engaged in a life-or-death struggle for their independence and survival. The accidents of conquest left them in possession of three separate mountainous areas west of the Jordan: Galilee, the central mountains, north of Jerusalem, and southern Judah. The cities of the Canaanites, some of them garrisoned with Egyptian mercenaries, continued to exist in the valleys of Jezreel and Harod, and they separated the northern from the central tribes. The enclave of Jerusalem-Jebus, which was left unconquered, divided the Rachel tribes of the centre from the Leah tribes of the south. In this divided state— for which the rise from time to time of charismatic leaders, the Judges, was no permanent remedy—the Israelites had to meet the formidable challenge of the Philistines.

The latter formed part of the great invasion of the 'Sea Peoples', who wrought havoc in the Eastern Mediterranean from Asia Minor to Egypt. The Philistines seem to have sojourned a long time within the orbit of the Minoan-Mycenaean culture of Crete and the Greek mainland. This is evidenced in part by their use of Greek names and titles (Achish, king of Gath = Anchises, the *seranim*, or lords of the Philistine pentapolis = tyrants). Their last stay seems to have been in Crete, for they are associated in the Bible with the Cretans (as in David's bodyguard of Cherethithes and Pelethites, i.e. Cretans and Philistines), and they also worshipped the Cretan god Marnas, who in due course became the chief god of Philistine Gaza. Philistine pottery, with its metope ornament filled with spirals, rhombs and images of swanlike birds, is a pale reflection of the close-knit and dynamic Mycenaean product.

The Philistines, characterized by their high feathered headdresses, which gives them some resemblance to American Indians, appear on Egyptian reliefs depicting battles with the 'Sea Peoples' in the reign of Rameses III, towards the end of the thirteenth century BC. They were turned back from Egypt, but occupied—probably with Egyptian connivance—the southern coastal plain, to which they gave the name of Philistia or Palestine, long before its extension to the whole of the country. They settled in five cities: Gaza, Ascalon (now Ashkelon), Ekron, Gath and Ashdod. The excavations of the last-named, in progress for several years, reveal a complex culture containing elements combining the Late Mycenaean and Canaanite civilizations. Among the finds at the Philistine levels are cult objects, such as seated figurines of gods, including a somewhat surrealistic representation of a woman shaped like a chair. There are numerous figurines of musicians, among these an incense stand with a group of players holding various instruments. At Beth Shean, which seems to have had a Philistine garrison (perhaps in Egyptian service) in the eleventh century BC, were found anthropoid pottery coffins, with representations of the high feathered headdresses of the Philistines.

Their iron weapons gave the Philistines a temporary superiority over the Israelites who were only armed with the old bronze swords and spear-heads (cf. *1 Samuel 13:19-22*). For a time the Philistines even established themselves on the watershed road in the central mountains;

◁
Aerial view of Bethlehem.

they maintained outposts at Gibeah in Benjamin (later Gibeath-Saul, now Tell el Ful, north of Jerusalem) and at Bethlehem. The excavations of the fortress at Gibeah, and of a city-gate at Ashdod, suggest strongly that what were regarded as two of the characteristic features of Israelite fortifications, the three-tongued gate and the casemate wall, were of Philistine origin.

As a small warrior class dominant over wide areas, the Philistines were unable to maintain their cultural integrity for any length of time; they adopted Canaanite writing and religion and finally disappeared in the mass of Hellenized Orientals in the third century BC.

Towards the end of the period of the Judges (in the middle of the eleventh century BC), the Israelites were hard pressed by these bold invaders from across the sea. In spite of the heroic exploits of Samson, his tribe of Dan was forced to leave its area close to the Philistine plain and to move northwards to the sources of the Jordan. It became clear that without a united national leadership, instead of the feeble high-priestly rule from Shiloh, the amphictyonic capital of tribal Israel, there would be no salvation for Israel. The first king, Abimelech, son of the judge Gideon, failed. The second, Saul, son of Kish, succeeded for a time, until defeated by the Philistines at the battle of Gilboa. David, son of Jesse, of Bethlehem, became the founder of a dynasty and the prototype of an Israelite king. He took Jerusalem and turned it into a national and religious centre by transferring there the Ark of the Covenant. Profiting from a power vacuum in the whole of the ancient Orient—for Egypt was enfeebled and Assyria not yet strong enough—he extended his power from the Brook of Egypt (Wadi el Arish) to the Euphrates, right across the Syrian desert. He controlled Damascus and the Aramaean states as well as Philistia and the three kingdoms east of the Jordan (Ammon, Moab and Edom), while carefully cultivating the friendship of the Phoenicians and the kings of Hamath, north of Damascus. Yet, although he laid the foundations of an empire, David left few tangible remains of his reign. The rock-cut tombs discovered at the southern tip of the Ophel hill of Jerusalem (the original 'Zion' or 'David's City') are possibly the remnants of the tombs of the Davidic dynasty for, like any king of his time, David claimed the privilege of being buried within his city, a right denied to lesser mortals.

At some time between the Hasmonaean revolt and the destruction of the Second Temple, a topographical revolution afflicted Jerusalem, the consequences of which are still echoed in popular beliefs today. For the Maccabees 'Mount Zion' was the Temple Mount, but by the time of Josephus it had been transferred to the Upper City, an area entirely outside the true Zion on the eastern hill. Before long a 'Tomb of David' was located there. The present monument, placed below the Coenaculum or site of the Last Supper, has as its north wall an apsidal structure, possibly part of a fourth-century synagogue. The cenotaph itself, which is nearly 4 m. long, is of Crusader workmanship; the outer shell of the building belongs to the Mameluke period. The 'Tomb of Absalom' is identified with the 'pillar in the King's Valley' (*2 Samuel 18:18*) which Absalom had set up for himself. The actual monument is connected with the nearby tomb-cave called 'Tomb of Jehoshaphat', and both date from the first century AD.

David's son Solomon (*c.* 970-930 BC) made peaceful moves in the wide area he inherited from his warrior father. In alliance with the Phoenicians he established a trade route from the Mediterranean to the Red

Anthropoid pottery coffin. The cover shows a human face and arms,
strongly stylized, possibly imitating Egyptian mummy coffins.
Early Iron Age (Philistine?). Rockefeller Museum.

Sea port of Elath and hence into Arabia and Africa. The wealth gained
in this way and the proceeds of heavy taxation enabled Solomon to
build his palace and the First Temple in Jerusalem. There is nothing
now left of these monuments, unless one considers as Solomonic a
small piece of walling excavated in 1966 just south of the south-eastern
corner of the Temple.
Outside Jerusalem the reign of Solomon has certainly left its mark.

According to the biblical account (*1 Kings 9:15*) he built the walls of Hazor and Megiddo and Gezer. It was exactly in these three sites that gates almost identical in plan ('made with the same blueprint' as some archaeologists are wont to say) have been discovered. They resemble the gates of Ashdod and consist of a portal leading into three successive courts, with four gateways; the gates are set within a casemate wall. As has been noted, it is quite likely that this plan of fortification was taken over from the Philistines. Other Solomonic buildings at Megiddo are a citadel near the wall, stables for his chariots (*Kings 9:19*)—although the large visible remains are of later date, a building of three rooms, with the central hall divided by two rows of pillars (perhaps a temple), a palace Solomon built on the Hittite *hilani* plan, with proto-Aeolic lotus capitals, and an administrative building with two courts and many small rooms. The fortress and temple at Arad are also attributed to Solomon in the first place. They correspond to a similar temple at Lachish, erected on the site of an earlier, Canaanite sanctuary. It is evident from these ruins that if Solomon was on the whole a worshipper of the God of Israel, this cult was by no means concentrated in Jerusalem.

After Solomon's death his kingdom fell apart; the two successor states, Israel in the north (which lasted till 721 BC) and Judah in the south (to 586 BC), were inversely proportional as regards material and religious importance. The northern kingdom was much more powerful and open to external influences; Judah remained traditional in its values and on a lower material level. It is typical that whereas in the north the kings and dynasties changed frequently, and usually with much violence, the south remained faithful to the Davidic dynasty—even if there also violence was not always absent. As regards religious life, which occupies the centre of the stage in the biblical account, the earlier prophets (Elijah, Elisha) were mainly active in Israel; but it was the later prophets whose words were recorded and who influenced future generations.

The capital of northern Israel was transferred from one locality to another until Omri, the most powerful of the kings of Israel, set it up in 880 BC at Samaria (Sebaste). His acropolis, surrounded with a casemate wall, covers an area of 25,000 square metres. The remaining segments of wall and the gate are built of well-cut ashlars, bossed in the centre, with a margin on three sides of the face. Within this area were found the Samaria *ostraca* (probably tax receipts from the eighth century) and remnants of the 'ivory house' (*Amos 3:15*) of Omri's successor, Ahab. Omri had married his son to the daughter of Ithbaal, king of the Sidonians, and opened his kingdom to Phoenician influences. The eclectic Phoenician art is evident in the Samarian ivories, mainly flat carved pieces which served as inlays in wooden furniture. Some of them reflect Egyptian art: lotus flowers, sphinxes, the god Harpocrates; others tend to use Mesopotamian patterns, as, for instance, the lion striking down a bull. The capitals from Megiddo and Hazor reflect the 'proto-Aeolic' lotus style.

Ahab, who was a relatively powerful king, secure in his alliance with Judah and Tyre, was able to face the Assyrians at the battle of Qarqar in 853 BC (the first certain date in biblical history), and to come off best. His activities are much in evidence at both Megiddo and Hazor, the great northern strongholds of his kingdom. At Hazor he constructed the great fortress on the upper tell (25 by 21 m., with walls 2 m. thick). In addition he built a large administrative building and cut the huge water-shaft. This descends to water level by a shaft and tunnel, both

Ivory carving of sphinx standing in a lotus thicket.
From the palace of Ahab at Samaria. Mid 9th century BC.
Rockefeller and Israel Museums.

provided with stairs; the total depth of the system is 40 m. The twisting staircase in the open shaft and the deep descent to water level in the tunnel give an idea of the impressive technical ability and geological knowledge of the engineers in the service of the kings of Israel in the ninth century BC. The works of Ahab at Megiddo are no less important than those at Hazor. They include the replacement of the Solomonic gate by one built on a different plan, with two courts and three wall-tongues and the replacement of the casemate wall by a broad wall alternating with projecting and re-entrant sections, a type of wall characteristic of the Late Israelite period. Other structures of Ahab at

Megiddo are the governor's palace and the two large stables in the northern and southern parts of the site. The stables consist of long rows of stone pillars with feeding and watering troughs in between. It must be remembered that in the battle of Qarqar, already mentioned, Ahab provided the largest contingent of chariots (2,000) of all the allies. The stables at Megiddo provided room for 450 horses, enough for 150 chariots. The water system at Megiddo is no less interesting than that at Hazor: a shaft with a staircase winding around it is followed by a straight tunnel, which reaches the water level of a source, direct access to which was blocked. In this way the inhabitants of Megiddo could obtain their water supply in time of siege, while the enemy outside would remain ignorant of its existence.

In the southern kingdom of Judah the water supply of the cities was no less carefully regulated than in the north. At Gezer and Lachish deep cuttings in the rock were made, although that at Lachish was abandoned before water was reached. Ancient Gibeon (el Jib) has two such systems: one consists of a deep pool (11.8 m. in diameter, 10.8 m. deep) with a rock-cut staircase winding along its sides. This might be the famous 'pool of Gibeon' mentioned in *2 Samuel 2:13*. From the pool a tunnel with 76 steps led down to the spring, 13.6 m. below. The cutting of the pool and tunnel required the removal of 3,000 tons of stone. Another tunnel with 93 steps was later added to this system. Jerusalem, which looms so large in history, was in eclipse while the northern kingdom of Israel was mighty; but in the time of Israel's decline, the southern monarchy began to expand. In the eighth and seventh centuries King Hezekiah of Judah (727-698 BC) cut a winding tunnel from the Gihon spring east of the City of David to a pool between the two hills on which stood Jerusalem (the 'Pool of Siloam'). About this time the city extended from the eastern to the western hill, into what was called 'the Second Jerusalem' (ha-Mishneh). The king built a wall 8 m. broad, in the later fashion—with bastions and inserts—across the western hill. This wall, found quite recently, has changed our views on the topography of Jerusalem. The tunnel of Hezekiah, through which the waters of the Gihon are still flowing into the pool, is a complicated piece of engineering. The inscription cut into the rock-wall of the tunnel, mentioned the great event of the 'Day of the Break-Through' when workers from both ends could hear each other's voices and 'the picks which struck one another'.

At Ramat Rahel, south of Jerusalem, a Judaean palace was built in the eighth century BC on a rectangular plan, with casemate walls sur-

rounding a court in which stood the palace itself and the attached buildings. Among the finds were the remains of a window balustrade of Phoenician shape, with proto-Aeolic capitals, some complete capitals and a sherd with the image of a bearded king, the only existing representation of a king of the Davidic dynasty.

In view of the importance given to it in the Scriptures, the religious life of the Israelite period is of special interest. We have already noted that until the time of Josiah, king of Judah (639-609 BC), the various local temples in Judah were active and were reconstructed from time to time. At Arad the temple is set within the north-eastern corner of the Israelite fortress and was maintained until dismantled by the zealot Josiah. A similar structure was found at Lachish. Both sanctuaries repeat the tripartite scheme of the Solomonic temple, with variations. They have an open court with an altar, a sanctuary and a holy of holies in the form of a separate room or niche. The porch is replaced by side rooms. In Arad, the incense altars were placed in the holy of holies, contrary to Jerusalem usage. All these Israelite temples were aniconic, as far as we know.

The temples, whether central or provincial, represent the official cult. Excavations in the private houses of the Israelite strata show an enormous quantity of figurines of idols, in particular the fertility goddess Astarte in the shape of a naked woman. The study of these figurines, in the field and even in museums, brings vividly to mind the strictures of the prophets against idolatry. Such representations of the Canaanite gods were taken over by the mass of the people from the former inhabitants; the incense stands of the Iron Age found at Beth Shean and Taanach, with their representations of idols of every kind, show how the traditional religions flourished contemporaneously with the belief in One God, as voiced by the prophets.

The first of these prophets, Elijah the Tishbite, was connected in particular with Mount Carmel. His contest with the priests of Baal (1 Kings 18) has been localized at el-Muhraqa, a prominent mountain top in the Carmel range, facing the Valley of Jezreel. Actually the site of the biblical story is not sufficiently clear. The evidence for a Baal of the Carmel, identical with the 'Lord of the Heavens' (Baal Saamin) and later with the Jupiter of Heliopolis (Baalbek), has been found on a votive foot of the Roman period, the dedication of one Gaius Iulius Eutyches of Caesarea (now in the Stella Maris Monastery). At the foot of Mount Carmel is a cave connected with the prophet since Roman-Byzantine times. More than 150 dedicatory inscriptions in Greek, Latin and Hebrew have been transcribed from its walls. The tradition goes back to the third century AD and probably even earlier.

The influence of the prophets was originally limited to those people who could listen to them in person. The earlier prophets, Elijah and Elisha and their schools, left no written records. Gradually, however, writing spread in Israel and Judah. The evidence for this remarkable phenomenon is supplied mainly by the *ostraca*, potsherds used as a cheap and handy substitute for papyrus. Used mostly for business documents, such as supply vouchers or tax receipts, these humble documents nevertheless give us much historic information. At Arad reference is made on an *ostracon* to the 'House of God', perhaps the Jerusalem temple; in another we learn of the rations issued to the foreign mercenaries of the kings of Judah; a third contains a reference to a threatening Edomite invasion. One long document, found on the coast and attributed to the time of Josiah, illustrates the depth to which the scriptural teachings had penetrated into popular consciousness. It is a letter of complaint, addressed to a governor, against the illegal forfeit of the cloak of a labourer in the *corvée* for nonfulfilment of his quota (cf. *Deut. 24:10-13*). Another piece of writing, the so-called Gezer calendar, possibly a school exercise, lists the months of the year and the agricultural tasks to be performed on each. The *ostraca* found at Lachish tell a dramatic story of the atmosphere in a Judaean fortress at the approach of Nebuchadnezzar's army in 587 BC when one fortress after another ceased to send signals because it had fallen. The inscription in a burial cave in Judah, *c.* 700 BC, contains a confrontation of two ideas prevalent when danger threatened from the Assyrians; the 'God of Jerusalem' to whom 'belongs the mountains of Judah' and who favours 'Mount Moriah, the dwelling place of Yah' is at the same time the 'God of the whole earth'.

Among the longer texts preserved we note (besides the tunnel inscription of Hezekiah already mentioned) the epitaphs of a 'royal steward', probably Shebna, a contemporary of Isaiah in the seventh century BC, which proclaimed, 'there is no silver and no gold here, but his bones and those of his slave-wife'. The seals found in the excavations also furnish vivid examples of the art and script of Iron Age Judah; the most famous of these are the seal of Shema, 'servant of Jeroboam' (II), found at Megiddo, with the picture of a roaring lion, and that of Jaazanaiah, 'servant of the king', found at Tell en-Nasbeh (Mizpeh of Gedaliah), which is adorned with the image of a rooster. This Jaazanaiah is probably mentioned in *2 Kings 25:23*. Also there is the seal of Jotham ('son of the King') with a device of Elath where he was governor.

Among the most common inscribed objects of the Judahite kingdom were the stamps found on handles of domestic jars; they depict a 'flying' or open scroll with the addition of the words *Lamelek* ('of', or 'belonging to', the King) and the name of one of four cities: Hebron, Zif, Socoh and another which may stand for Jerusalem. It is still unclear whether these stamps indicate a royal measure (there is a parallel inscription '*Bat* [a liquid measure] *lamelekh*') or whether they indicate that the jars were made in a royal pottery or were destined for taxes in kind. The seals, decorated with images, bring us to the art of Iron Age

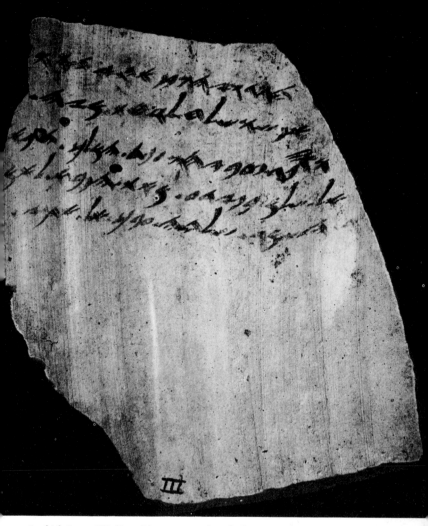

Lachish Letter III. Found in gateway of Lachish destroyed in 587/6 BC
*by the Babylonians. The letters are addressed to the governor of Lachish by
Hoshaiah, an army officer. Rockefeller Museum.*

Israel. In general, apart from some examples from Judah, these objects do not reveal a rigid adherence to the stricter interpretation of the Second Commandment: men appear occasionally, beasts frequently. If this is the case in orthodox Judah, the northern kingdom of Israel was even more lax. There Phoenician influences dominated, as is evidenced by the ivories found at Samaria and by the capitals there and at Megiddo. The relatively high standard of figurative art in the Iron Age can be explained by the economic activity of those times. The excavations in Engeddi have supplied us with ample evidence of a prosperous economy. A royal perfume factory was located at Engeddi and perfume vats have been discovered there on the terraces before the houses. A heap of silver pieces, forerunners of a regular currency, was also found. Glimpses of the domestic life of the period are further afforded by the figurines from Phoenician tombs found at Achzib north of Acre: a woman in her bath, another baking, a man anointing a sacred pillar with oil. Pottery models found in various sites illustrate the domestic furniture of the time. At Gibeon an immense wine store was found, calculated to hold 95,000 litres of wine; the *ostraca* found there record the names of the various proprietors of this the vineyards.

The Israelite tombs followed the Phoenician type in some cases, with a deep shaft leading to the tomb-chamber cut in the rock, and a monument (*nefesh*) above it. Another type of tomb was borrowed from the Egyptians and imitated the pyramids, but on a very much smaller scale. The famous Kidron valley necropolis facing Jerusalem on the east was begun in the Iron Age with the so-called 'Tomb of Pharaoh's Daughter'—a rock-cut monolithic cube surmounted by an Egyptian *cyma* and, at one time, by a pyramid. This and the tomb called the 'Monolith Tomb' represent the only monuments of the Iron Age left standing in this area.

The tangible material remains of the Israelite period are not commensurate with its spiritual significance for future ages. This was due mainly to the length and material development of the succeeding periods, which effectively covered up the earlier remains. The effects of a profound spiritual revolution also were frequently destructive rather than constructive. If some of the local 'high places' (*bamoth*) west of Jerusalem were destroyed by Josiah or the temple at Arad dismantled, the monotheistic idea apparent behind such acts was hardly to be seen there.

Nevertheless the Israelite period was one of decisive importance in the history of the Holy Land. The earlier compromises with the local Canaanite fertility cults were abandoned as soon as the people became convinced of the truth of the prophetic message. This was made evident by the scourging of Israel and Judah by Assyria and Babylonia. These disasters, which were foretold, not only prepared the ground for monotheism, which recognized only One God as true, all the others being false, but they also laid the foundation for obedience to the divine law in daily life which characterized later Judaism. Moreover the part of the prophetic message which was addressed to the moral feelings of the people, as opposed to institutionalized religion (priests, sacrifices, even the Temple), was soon overshadowed by the lofty Messianic ideal addressed to all nations. The vision of the latter days when 'swords shall be beaten into plough shares...nation shall not lift up its sword against nation... neither shall they learn war any more', which still remains the loftiest ideal of mankind, originated in the words of Isaiah, a prophet in Judah in the Israelite period.

Persians, Macedonians and Greeks

The fall of Jerusalem to Nebuchadnezzar in 586 BC was followed by the exile of the major part of the Jewish nation to Babylonia, leaving in Judah only the 'poorest of the land', 'vinedressers and ploughmen' (*2 Kings 25:12*). After fifty years, Cyrus, king of Persia, overthrew the New Babylonian empire and established his rule over the Orient. In line with his policy of religious restoration, he allowed the Jews to return from exile and to rebuild the Temple. The country was very poor, and despite assistance from the Babylonian exiles the work went on with great slowness, complicated by Samaritan intrigues and Persian bureaucracy. The Second Temple was finally dedicated in 519 BC.

Persian Judah was very different from the Judah in the period before the exile. The high-priests, beginning with Jeshua, son of Jozadak, became the heads of the Jewish nation. Civil power was in the hands of a Persian governor, usually a Jew, who was subject to the Persian satrap of Ebirnari, the 'Land beyond the River' (Euphrates), residing at Damascus. Only very gradually did the Judaeans free themselves from

Pottery mask from Phoenician tombs at Achzib (ez Zib) north of Acre.
Probably the apotropaic representation of a goddess. Iron Age.
Rockefeller Museum.

the tutelage of the governor and nobles of Samaria. The decisive step was taken by Nehemiah, son of Hacaliah, who rebuilt the walls of Jerusalem and thus safeguarded the Holy City from attack by its northern neighbours. This made possible the thorough religious reform of Ezra the Scribe, who established with success the 'Rule of the Divine Law', henceforth characteristic of Jewish culture.

One result of Persian rule was the gradual extension of the use of Aramaic among the Jews. The Persians used one form (the so-called 'imperial Aramaic') as the official language of the western part of the empire, and the documents of the Jewish communities in the Diaspora are written in that language. Even the official name of Judah was now the Aramaic Yehud. Thus the name of the province was written on its silver coins, which imitate the Athenian silver drachmae, with the symbol of the owl. Yehud appears also on numerous stamps of jar handles, together with the name of Jerusalem (or 'the City', ha-'ir) and the names of some officials (the peha or governor, and the treasurer). Many of these seals come from the administrative headquarters excavated at Ramat Rahel, south of Jerusalem. The palace there survived the fall of Jerusalem and was an administrative centre in Persian times, probably as the secondary headquarters of the Jerusalem district.

North of Judaea was the land of the Samaritans. These mixed people were the descendants of settlers brought to Samaria by the Assyrian kings after the fall of the kingdom of Israel, as part of their policy of resettling the conquered peoples. The new settlers intermingled with the remnants of the Israelites and worshipped the same God; they used the old Hebrew writing and established a centre of worship on Mount Gerizim, served by priests who had broken with the Jerusalem priestly families. The strict legitimist policy of Ezra and the Jewish reformers denied them their share in the Second Temple, and a rift developed between the Jews and Samaritans which was to mark the history of both almost till the present day.

The Persian period also witnessed great changes in the coastal plain. Because of their naval importance the Persian kings favoured the Phoenician cities, and granted them large areas in the fertile lands extending from Mount Carmel south. Here the Tyrians and Sidonians established landing places and settlements. Two such sites, those of Athlith and Tell Megadim, have been excavated, the latter recently. The city has a rectangular plan, with a west wall 170 m. long, and north and south walls of 100 m. each. Streets run parallel with the walls.

At Athlith the finds included a settlement and graves of what appears to be a colony of Greek mercenaries, who had clearly taken native wives, for the arms and seals found were Greek and Macedonian, while the trinkets, mirrors and amulets were Oriental, mostly Egyptian. This site and that of Tell Gamma (Jemmeh) further south are rich in Greek, especially Attic, painted pottery. They indicate an important new cultural strain from the West, which then began to make its mark upon the country.

Greek mercenaries had already appeared in this country in the time of King Josiah, in the seventh century; but in the Persian period they became much more numerous, serving both the Greek king and the Egyptians who rebelled against him. The famous victories of Marathon, Plateae and Eurymedon had convinced all the rulers of the East of the superiority of the Greek as a fighting man. The naval defeats at Salamis and elsewhere thwarted the attempts of the Phoenicians in

Persian service to keep the eastern basin of the Mediterranean as an area closed to Greek ships. Besides the mercenaries, Greek travellers and merchants appeared in the East—the most famous traveller being Herodotus who, passing along the coast from Egypt northwards, remarked on the 'Palestinian' Syrians (meaning the Philistines) and in so doing originated the name of Palestine. Owing to the maritime character of their commerce, the influence of the Greeks was most evident in the coastal area; there is some reason to believe that one of the coastal cities, Dor, even became a member of the Athenian Maritime League; in the territorial division of this alliance which was originally directed against Persia, it was included in the section comprising the cities of Caria in southern Asia Minor. In any case the influence of Attic coinage, the standard silver, coin of international commerce, can be seen in the 'Philisto-Arabian' coins struck, probably by the local rulers to pay their mercenaries; but it even reached inland Judaea, as we have seen. However, most of the local culture remained Oriental in the Persian period, as can be seen in the Tell Sharuhen silver spoon and bowl.

Persian rule over the Orient ended suddenly with the lightning conquests of Alexander the Great. The battle of Issus (332 BC) ended Persian domination over Phoenicia and Palestine. The sieges of Tyre and Gaza made the new rule secure. Alexander himself forged down the coast to Egypt and in 331 BC marched back towards Babylonia. His rule was too brief and too tumultuous to make any lasting changes, except perhaps the settlement of Macedonian mercenaries at Samaria as a punishment for a Samaritan revolt. During the years after Alexander's death warfare between his successors was incessant; from

Slab of black granite with inscription in Greek, with Hellenistic lettering. From Samaria, c. 3rd century BC. Rockefeller Museum.

301 BC onwards the Holy Land was firmly in the hands of Ptolemy I
Soter, the king of Egypt. With Ptolemaic rule the Hellenistic period
might be said properly to have begun.

Hellenism had already begun to influence local culture in the Persian
period and its importance was greatly enhanced when the administration, at least in its upper levels, passed into Greek hands. The tremendous energy of the Greeks in the Orient was directed mainly
towards economic development. The replacement of a Persian governor
by a Greek did not matter as much as the fact that the country was
overrun by agents of the finance minister of the Ptolemies, always
on the lookout for new enterprises to be started and new settlements
to be made. In Palestine proper there was little room for a Greek
colony—apart from Samaria which was settled by Macedonian veterans.
There was much more to be done east of the Jordan and in the Jordan
valley itself. This area, previously settled only in a few oases, was now
provided with irrigation channels running down from the mountains. It
became exceedingly prosperous because of the combination of fertile
soil, ample sunshine and water.

Economic life was given a further fillip through the release of hoards
of Persian gold and silver by Alexander and his successors. The
quickened pulse of the economy was turned to good advantage by the
Phoenicians, always the best merchants in the Levant. The Phoenician
capitals, Tyre and Sidon, having become independent cities, now lost
their hold on the whole coast. But the entire area from Gaza to
Accho now adopted Greek culture to a large extent, and shared in
the new prosperity of the Hellenistic age. Accho became Ptolemaic
and remained such until the Arab conquest. Further inland, the Ptolemies settled some of their Scythian mercenaries at Beth Shean and
called the settlement Scythopolis.

We get a vivid picture of the state of Palestine in 259 BC from the
letters of Zenon, an agent of the Ptolemaic finance minister Apollonius,
who crossed the country from Straton's Tower (Herodian Caesarea) to
Jerusalem and Jericho. Zenon corresponded with the Greek officials
scattered over the country. One of their headquarters was Marissa
(Maresha) in Idumaea. Originally inhabited by Edomites (Idumaeans)
who migrated there from southern Trans-Jordan after the exile of the
Judaeans to Babylonia, Marissa became a Hellenized township under
the Ptolemies. The excavations at its Hellenistic level show the typically
rationalistic city plan evolved by the Greek Hippodamus—streets
crossing at right angles, with a space reserved for public buildings and
the market place. Tombs of the Hellenized Sidonians settled at Marissa
have been excavated. They were painted with animal friezes based
on the zoological handbooks of the Hellenistic period. Interest in natural
science was one of the characteristics of that age; the Ptolemaic kings
kept a zoo at Alexandria, with rare animals from central Africa. Some
of these found their place at Marissa. Another monument of the Hellenistic period which reflects concern with security is the round tower
that once formed part of the city-wall of Samaria. Built of rows of
headers, it illustrates the scientific architectural technique of the period.
Its existence demonstrates the feeling of insecurity which haunted the

▷

Terracotta figurine of Aphrodite. From Mount Carmel. Hellenistic Period.
Rockefeller Museum.

Greeks in the East, a minority settled among millions of natives who maintained their own traditions.

In religious matters the Greeks in the Orient capitulated before the gods of the East at an early stage. Inscriptions from Samaria, dating from the beginning of the Hellenistic settlement, are dedicated to the Egyptian gods Serapis and Isis, and only rarely to the traditional Olympic deities. A temple of the Hellenistic period has been found at Scythopolis, dedicated to Dionysos. It is by no means certain to what extent the Greek gods were worshipped in the East as such, or whether they merely lent their names and shapes to Oriental deities. The figurine of Aphrodite found in a cave at Athlith, inscribed to the goddess by a certain Paeonias (the dedication can also be read 'Paeonias is very happy') clearly shows the influence of the great fourth-century sculptor Praxiteles. Another piece of Hellenistic sculpture is a marble head found at Beth Shean, possibly an image of Alexander the Great, who was worshipped as a god by the Oriental Greeks. His image also appears on the beautiful Hellenistic coins struck at Ptolemais, Jaffa and Gaza by the Ptolemies and their successors, the Seleucids.

The material culture of the Hellenistic period reached a very high standard as a result of economic activity and social change. Hundreds of wine-jars, their handles stamped with the date and name of the eponymous priest or merchant, give evidence of the volume of exports from the great commercial centre of Rhodes, which supplied all the East with Greek wines. Other fine Hellenistic wares are the 'Megarian' bowls, of pottery decorated in relief with floral ornaments and mythological scenes; their true origin is as yet unknown, but could possibly be Asia Minor or Antioch. The technique of pressing such vessels in negative moulds was also applied to glass vessels, and replaced the old method of winding glass thread around a sand-core. Toward the end of the Hellenistic period glass-blowing was invented and spread rapidly. According to a Greek story, the use of glass was invented accidentally in the dunes south of Ptolemais-Acre; in any case the Phoenician coast soon became full of glass factories and exporters.

Hellenistic wares were probably the prototypes of a new kind of pottery culture which became prominent towards the end of the Hellenistic period. Its carriers were the Nabateans, a desert tribe which moved into the area vacated by the Edomites in southern Trans-Jordan. They established their capital at Petra, repulsed attacks by Antigonus the One-Eyed, one of Alexander's successors, and extended their rule over the Negev wilderness. Remains of Nabatean buildings are still visible at Avdat (Eboda), the burial place of their deified king Obodas III. His successor Arethas IV (9 BC - AD 40) erected a temple in honour of Zeus Obodas; the platform and staircases leading to this edifice have been preserved. At Kurnub (Mamshit, Mampsis) Nabatean palaces are still standing to the second floor, complete with staircases and stables. On a multitude of sites in the Negev, and as far north as Caesarea, Nabatean pottery has been identified, easily recognizable by its egg-shell thinness and stylized floral designs.

Hellenization, which was pursued prudently by the Ptolemies, received a powerful impetus when Palestine passed into the hands of their Seleucid rivals, beginning with Antiochus III (198 BC). His son

▷

Aerial view of Avdat, a Nabatean town in the Negev.

Site of the Acra fortress, seen opposite the Temple Mount in the Old City, Jerusalem. Erected by Antiochus IV 'Epiphanes', it remained a Syrian stronghold till it was taken by Simeon the Hasmonaean in 143 BC.

Antiochus IV Epiphanes ('God manifest', changed into *Epimanes*, 'the Madman', by his enemies), tried to unify his kingdom culturally and religiously, in order to make a stand against the Roman power which had humbled his father at Magnesia in 189 BC. He also tried to force Hellenization on the Jews and was encouraged in this enterprise by the Hellenizers among them. The strife which arose in Judaea led to disturbances at the very moment when Antiochus was engaged in conquering Egypt. In order to safeguard his rear defenses he occupied Jerusalem and, at the request of the Hellenizers, set up a Greek city (Antioch) besides the Jewish town. A fortress, the Acra, was built over the Temple. The king was persuaded to apply the usual method of syncretization to the God of Israel and to identify Zebaoth 'Lord of Hosts' with Dionysos Sabazius. The Temple was desecrated and sacrifices ceased for three and a half years (167-164 BC). Antiochus IV was not satisfied with this but prepared to erect a huge temple (probably dedicated to the Olympic Zeus, his favourite deity) near the Acra. A column base and an Ionic capital which seem to have belonged to this temple have recently been found in the old city of Jerusalem.

Misled by his advisers, who predicted a prompt Hellenization of the Jews, Antiochus IV tried to suppress Jewish religious practices and thus gained the doubtful honour of starting the first religious persecution in history. He thereby provoked the Hasmonaean revolt.

The Hasmonaeans

The Hasmonaean revolt broke out in the small town of Modiin (el-Midye) on the Judaean border. It was led by the priest Mathathias and his five sons, the most prominent of whom was Judas Maccabaeus. Gathering around him the bands of the 'Pious' (Assidaeans), Judas was able to defeat four Seleucid armies, one after another, which hastened to relieve the Jerusalem Acra, blockaded by the insurgents. After the fourth battle, that of Beth Zur, Judas and his men occupied the Temple Mount and proceeded to purify the Temple. Worship was resumed in December 164 BC, an event commemorated at the Feast of Dedication (Hannukkah) to this day.

The struggle between Judas and his followers on the one side and the Seleucid government and its adherents on the other continued with varying fortunes till 152 BC. In that year Jonathan the Hasmo-naean (who had commanded the insurgents after Judas's death on the battlefield of Eleasa, 163 BC) was appointed high-priest and governor of Judaea. As such he was practically independent, although the Hel-lenizers and the Seleucid garrisons still remaining at the Jerusalem Acra and Beth Zur constituted a serious limitation to his freedom. The presence of enemies in the heart of his dominions obliged Jonathan to fortify Jewish Jerusalem. Remains of his wall and tower are still standing on the Ophel hill south of the Old City. Other walls protected the City of David, then in Jewish hands, against the western hill ('Mount Zion' today) which was in the hands of the enemy.

Jonathan's successor Simeon, last of the five Hasmonaean brothers, achieved complete independence for Judaea, as 'high-priest, prince and commander-in-chief' rolled into one. He obtained the capitulation of the Acra; on 23rd of Iyar 143 BC this 'great enemy was destroyed out of Israel' (*1 Maccabees 13:51*). He also seized the fortress of Beth Zur and established his own men there. The ruins of the Hellenistic fortress have been excavated at this site (31 x 41 m.); strong outer walls and a courtyard surrounded by living rooms have been revealed. Another of Simeon's conquests was that of the important fortress of Gezer situated on the Jerusalem-Jaffa road. The capture of this stronghold was effected by means of a siege tower (*helepolis* in Greek), a sophisticated machine operated by the Hasmonaean army. In general this period marks the achievement by the armies of Jonathan and Simeon of military equality with the Greek phalanxes, an advantage which was soon to be used to enlarge the boundaries of Judaea. In Gezer the Hasmonaeans made use of the earlier Solomonic fortifications. They turned the fortress into a military camp second only to Jerusalem. Simeon employed prisoners of war in the building of his stronghold there. An inscription scribbled by one of these forced labourers, 'May fire burn Simeon's house', has been found in the excavations of Gezer.

Simeon's son, John Hyrcanus (134-104 BC), and his grandsons, Judah Aristobulus (104-103 BC) and Jonathan (Alexander Jannaeus 103-76 BC), gradually conquered the whole of Palestine, taking one Greek city after another. They were also engaged in a continuous struggle with the Seleucid and Ptolemaic rulers and other Oriental nations. In the course of this process of expansion Idumaea and Galilee became entirely

*Hasmonaean walls uncovered inside the court
of the Jerusalem citadel, part of the first wall of Jerusalem.*

Jewish, while the Samaritans kept their identity. In these struggles the character of the Hasmonaean kingdom (for Aristobulus and Jannaeus had adopted the title of king) was greatly changed. The Hasmonaean revolt began as a rising against the Hellenistic world and all that it implied; in the course of time, however, the Hasmonaean rulers were forced to adopt many of the Hellenistic innovations in the field of administration and warfare; they could not otherwise have withstood their enemies and extended their power. Alexander Jannaeus, who was the most tireless warrior of the dynasty, even employed foreign mercenaries to wage war. This Hellenizing tendency of the dynasty brought about a dangerous inner division in the Jewish nation. Against the kings and their adherents, the Sadducees, rose the popular party of the Pharisees, who demanded a separation of the religious function (the high-priesthood) from the civil (the royalty). Matters eventually came to a head and civil war broke out between the king and the Pharisees, in which the Jewish rebels, allied with a Seleucid king, fought a pitched battle with a Jewish king supported by Greek mercenaries. In the end Jannaeus got the upper hand; some of his enemies fled and others he executed. Still fighting, he died in his camp before the fortress of Ragaba, which his army was besieging and which fell after his death.

Few material remains survived the stormy period of the Hasmonaeans, and these are mostly connected with warlike events. Having occupied the site of the ill-starred 'Antioch-by-Jerusalem' (the western of the two hills of old Jerusalem), the Hasmonaeans took care to encircle it with a strong wall. Remains of these fortifications are still visible in the citadel. It is constructed of headers in the Hellenistic style (as is the Samaria tower), but the single stones are provided

Left of the wall are the foundations of Herod's palace.
Crusader and Mameluke walls of the present day citadel (below and right).

Porch of the Tomb of the Bene Hezir ('Tomb of St James'), Jerusalem.

with a boss and a margin in the style of the old Israelite ashlar dressing. More fragments of this wall were found near Gobat's school on 'Mount Zion' and near the Siloam Pool. On Mount Sartaba, overlooking the Jordan valley, Jannaeus constructed the fortress of Alexandrium; it remained one of the main strongholds of the Hasmonaean kingdom and played a most important role in the wars and revolts that marked the decline of the dynasty. Here too the wall shows the same boss and margin, on moderate sized stones, as in the Jerusalem citadel. A third Maccabean fortress was Hyrcania (Khirbet el Mird, Byzantine Castellion) in the Judaean desert where today there are remains of a fortress and an aqueduct. The fourth of Jannaeus' fortresses, Masada, was altered by King Herod to such an extent that almost no Maccabean remains are visible.

In the Jerusalem citadel another historical event of the Hasmonaean period has left its traces: the wall was breached (probably during the siege of Antiochus VII Sidetes) and repaired in haste.

The Hasmonaean coinage provides valid evidence of the changes in the state of mind of the rulers of the second sovereign Jewish commonwealth. The earliest coins, struck by John Hyrcanus, show on one side the Hellenistic symbol of two horns of plenty, but the

Pyramidal monument ('Tomb of Zechariah') of the Bene Hezir mausoleum.

caduceus of Hermes, which appears on Greek coins between the two commonwealths, was replaced by the innocuous pomegranate. On the obverse the Seleucid kings always put their portrait. As this would be contrary to the rigorous interpretation of the Second Commandment, common in Hasmonaean times, the head of the ruler was replaced by his name and titles, written in the old Hebrew script within a wreath. The formula 'John—or Judah or Jonathan—high-priest and head of the Heber (*Koinon*) of the Jews' marked the constitutional position of the Hasmonaean rulers who had been entrusted with power by the people in the days of Simeon. When Jannaeus decided to change his status in relation to the people, he replaced the old symbols with the star (symbol of luck) and the anchor, a sign of his rule over the coast and its harbours. He also changed the inscription to 'Jonathan/Alexander King' in Hebrew and in Greek, and thus introduced a regal era. It seems that towards the end of his reign, when he had made peace with the people, he reverted to the old style of coinage.

Of the Hasmonaean palaces on the site of the Acra in Jerusalem only a few architectural ruins remain, together with a relief showing the same symbol as that found on the coins: two horns of plenty with a pomegranate between them—perhaps the arms of the Hasmonaean state.

Two monumental tombs still standing in Jerusalem provide the best evidence of prevailing artistic style. One of them is situated in the Kidron Valley necropolis and was the burial place of a priestly family called Bene Hezir, which is attested by an inscription on its façade.

The traditional name 'Tomb of St James' is no more true in this case than in that of the so-called 'Tomb of Absalom' or 'Tomb of Zechariah', but in the case of the Bene Hezir tomb the actual name of the people buried there is known. The tomb façade is of a severe and almost classical Doric style; the monolith cut out of the rock, usually called 'Tomb of Zechariah', was probably once the 'monument' or 'mark' (*nefesh*) attached to the Hezir tomb. Within the tomb we find the classical scheme of the Jerusalem necropolis: a central hall follows the porch, with three rooms spreading from it; each room has a depression in the centre and several burial places (*kokhim, loculi*) cut in the wall. The second tomb of the Hasmonaean period, found untouched (the Kidron Valley tombs were all plundered ages ago), was that of one Jason and his family. Archaeological evidence dates this tomb to the time of Alexander Jannaeus. The monument stands in Alfasi Road, Jerusalem. It is approached by a passage, ending in a small court. The façade is divided by a single column, with doors on either side and there is a moulding around the entrance. The whole edifice is surmounted by a pyramid. In the porch were found drawings of a sea-battle; Jason was probably one of the captains under Jannaeus who fought Greek ships. These captains were regarded as naval heroes by the Jews and sa pirates by the Greek cities. Within the tomb there was a burial chamber and a bone chamber. The tomb marks the transition from the family-type burial of the Sadducee tradition (which followed the Bible) to the individual burial practised by the Pharisees, who believed in the resurrection of every human being.

Qumran and the Dead Sea Sect

The religious turmoil of the Hasmonaean period produced not only the great split between the Sadducees and the Pharisees (the political and the religious authorities) and between the Hellenizers and the followers of the old traditions. There were also many minor splinter groups and sects who separated from the body of the nation. One of these minor sects has become famous in our time through the discovery of many documents relating to it in the caves around the ruins of Qumran, north of the Dead Sea.

The founder of this sect was known to its adherents only by his title: the Teacher or Master of Justice. He came into conflict with the 'Wicked Priest', who had him executed. His followers retreated to 'Damascus'—whether this means the real city or a symbolic refuge in the desert is not known. In any case, the sect settled on the site of Qumran, and remained there until the destruction of the site in the First Jewish Revolt, in AD 68. There was one period during which the place was left deserted, but after this interruption the same group of persons who had founded Qumran resumed residence there. In the caves around the site hundreds of papyrus fragments of writing were found, including the first find of seven scrolls in cave No. 1. The attention of the learned world was drawn to the sect and its activities through the discovery of these documents in 1947. One of the documents, the so-called 'Zadokite Document' (or 'Damascus Document'),

◁
Caves outside the Qumran monastery in which one of the first seven scrolls of the Dead Sea Sect were found by a Bedouin shepherd in 1947.

had been known for several generations, a copy of it having been found in the Cairo Geniza in 1896-97; but it was only the Qumran finds which placed it in its proper context.

From these documents a picture emerges of a tightly organized religious community, headed by priests and Levites, together with selected laymen. The priests derived their status from the House of Zadok, the priestly family of David's time. The Dead Sea sect rejected the 'upstart' priests of the Hasmonaean dynasty. They also rejected the Temple in Jerusalem and put their faith in a future Temple of greater purity. They adopted a calendar based on a different system from that used by the rest of the Jews and in this way separated themselves in perpetuity from the others, keeping holy the days regarded as working days by the rest, and working on the holy days kept by the others. The main body consisted of members who had passed a period of probation and who had surrendered their property to be administered by overseers on behalf of the community, which included women and children. The male members had their meals in common; they sat in order of rank, which was reassessed every year.

The tenets of the community, as far as they can be understood from its writings, included a belief that they were the 'Chosen of the Lord' and that all those not elected were to perish for ever. The fact of election was a matter of divine predestination and not liable to change. They believed that the end of the world was near and their writings include a scroll describing the 'War of the Sons of Light [themselves] with the Sons of Darkness', which would end, of course, with the victory of the Light. How far this War Manual represents real training for fighting and how far it is a mere apocalyptic speculation is still a matter of dispute. As befitted the exalted character of the sect, they laid special stress on the books of the Bible which suited their spiritual aspiration, such as the *Book of Isaiah*, the *Psalms* and the *Minor Prophets*. In any case they interpreted these biblical texts in the light of contemporary events. As the allusions in the commentaries were veiled, their chronological background is not clear to modern scholars. Among the documents of the sect were 'Thanksgiving Hymns' composed by its members, in which its doctrines are set forth in the language of the orthodox Psalms. The documents also included two copper scrolls containing lists of fabulous treasures hidden in the vicinity of Jerusalem, in the Judaean desert and in other places. Whether these lists represent real treasures or are simply the fruit of an exuberant fantasy is a matter for conjecture.

The historical background of the rise of the sect is by no means clear. Excavations at Qumran have established that the settlement already existed in the days of John Hyrcanus. Clearly the separation between the sect and the rest of the nation took part in Hasmonaean times. This would cast either Simeon or his son John (more likely the former) in the role of the 'Wicked Priest'. Possibly the dual assumption of the high priesthood and of temporal rule provoked the secession of the Qumran sect. It seems to have lingered on until the time of Herod, when the king, himself an outcast and favouring others in a similar position, appears to have encouraged them to settle in Jerusalem. They seem to have returned to Qumran in the time of Archelaus, Herod's son, and to have stayed on in this 'Stronghold of the Pious' (*Mezad Hassidim*) till its destruction by the Romans, who did not distinguish between the various Jewish sects.

It is more or less generally agreed that the Qumran sect was identical with the Essenes, described in the writings of Josephus and Pliny,

Monastery of the Dead Sea Sect near the seashore. In the background can be seen the road leading to Masada.

although their accounts do not absolutely correspond to what we know of it. Members of the Qumran sect, like the Essenes, seem to have taken part in the war with the Romans. Fragments of their writings have been found among the remains of the Zealots encamped at Masada.

The relationship between the Qumran sect and early Christianity is less clear. There are certain verbal concordances between parts of the New Testament and some of the Qumran texts. It seems safest to regard both religious movements as part of the general ferment which troubled the Jewish nation at the end of the first century BC.

The remains of Qumran, the seat of the sect, were excavated in 1956-61. They include a main building, square in plan, with a strong tower at its north-western corner. The central court is surrounded by rectangular rooms, among which have been identified a council chamber with benches along its walls, a scriptorium, where the scribes sat who copied the texts of the Bible and writings of the sect, a kitchen, and other rooms. A large dining hall was added on the south side of the complex, with a potter's workshop and a storehouse near by. A further extension included a sheepfold. The site, situated in the desert near Jericho, was supplied with water from an aqueduct running from nearby mountains. The ruins include no less than eight pools, most of them rectangular in shape and provided with steps. The ritual of the sect called for very frequent ablutions, and ample provision was made for these. In one of the pools can be seen 'clear traces of an earthquake, probably that of AD 31'. A score of caves have been found all around the ruin, many of them containing fragments of scrolls, while others were used for dwelling purposes. A camping site outside the 'monastery' of Qumran indicates that not all members of the sect dwelt within its walls. About one thousand plain tombs of members of the sect were found in the vicinity.

The Reign of King Herod

While the Qumran sect was living in its desert retreat, the rule of the hated Hasmonaeans was coming to an end. The two sons of Alexander Jannaeus, Aristobulus II and Hyrcanus II, were engaged in a fratricidal war, when the Roman general Pompey appeared in Judaea. After taking the Temple by force, he decided in favour of Hyrcanus II, the weaker one (63 BC), and Judaea thus lost its independence. Within one generation the last of the Hasmonaeans had been dethroned and his

Rock-cuttings in the northwest corner of the temple esplanade, Jerusalem, remnants of the Herodian Antonia fortress. Muslim buildings of the Mameluke period, including el-Madrasa el-Jawliya on left, on top of them.

place taken by the Idumaean Herod, the son of Antipater, who had already administered the country under Hyrcanus II.

Herod had been appointed king of the Jews at Rome in 40 BC while his rival Antigonus, the last Hasmonaean king, still ruled in Jerusalem by the grace of the Parthian invaders. It took him three years of fighting and a bloody siege of Jerusalem to become king in reality. He reigned for 33 years, and died a painful death at Jericho. After his death he was recorded in the Gospels as 'King Herod', who had had the children of Bethlehem massacred.

Actually Herod was a most energetic and successful ruler, even if he could not master the circumstances of his time. Placed by the grace of the Romans on his throne in Jerusalem, he was hated by his Jewish subjects, and tolerated by the Greeks under his dominion. Herod's aim, once his rule was secure under the protection of the emperor Augustus (31 BC - AD 14), was to avoid a conflict between Jews and Romans and to bring the former as near as possible to the dominant Graeco-Roman culture. Following a prudent financial policy he disposed of great treasures, which he used to secure his capital and kingdom in order to gain the goodwill or at least the tolerance of his Jewish subjects, and to dazzle the Greeks of the East. In Jerusalem Herod built himself a splendid palace in the north-western sector of the city (now near the citadel); the palace was protected on the northern side by three strong towers, called after his brother Phasael, a friend Hippicus, and his wife Mariamme. Of the three, only the foundations of Phasael are still standing as the traditional 'Tower of David' at

Jerusalem. The base measures 20 m. square and 20 m. in height; it forms a solid block of masonry. The big stones show the characteristic dressing of the Herodian period: a flat low boss surrounded a narrow margin, with another broader and shallower margin around it. Herod's palace was encircled by a separate wall; it faced the Upper Market, the central square of the Upper City, seat of the high priests and their families, the local aristocracy. This quarter, the former Hellenistic 'Antioch', was separated from the rest of the city by a wall on its eastern side. It included the remains of the old Hasmonaean palace, redecorated with Corinthian capitals and frescoes, some of which have been found in recent excavations in the Jewish quarter of the Old City. Another of Herod's fortresses in Jerusalem was named by him 'Antonia' in honour of the triumvir Mark Antony. Remains of its walls and possibly of its pavement (the Lithostrotos mentioned in the New Testament as the place where Jesus was judged) are still visible in the Convent of Our Lady of Zion in the Old City. Below the pavement are the twin pools called Struthion (Ostrich?), mentioned by Josephus in connexion with the 'Antonia'.

Herod's mightiest undertaking was the enlargement of the Temple Mount by doubling its surface, and the complete reconstruction of the Temple itself. Of the latter building nothing visible remains; but the western, southern, and part of the eastern walls of Herod's esplanade are still standing above ground. In the excavations conducted by B. Mazar since 1968 the Herodian street pavement and steps have been unearthed south of the Temple. The face of the wall is constructed of huge stones, 10-12 m. long, set in the corners alternately as headers and stretchers. Each layer is about 1 m. high. A high arch, 12 m. above the street and 15 m. wide (the so-called 'Robinson's Arch'), joined the Temple wall with a building across the street. Another arch ('Wilson's Arch'), further north, led to the Upper City. Between the two arches is the Jewish praying area, known in Hebrew as the 'Western Wall' (*Kotel Maaravi*) and in European languages as the 'Wailing Wall'. The wall continues underground northwards. The monumental effect of Herod's wall is tremendous; it should be remembered that the walls at present visible were surmounted by a high structure with attached pillars, such as can still be seen in the Herodian wall round the Machpelah cave in Hebron, and that they descended in places 25 m. down to the rock. There were four gates in the west wall, two in the south, and one each in the north and east.

Below the Temple wall extended a Herodian street with steps leading up to the Double (south) gates of the Temple. At Hebron the Herodian walls round the Machpelah cave are still standing almost to their full height and they give us an idea of how the Jerusalem enclosure must have looked. Two finds from the Jewish quarter of the Old City illustrate the style of the period: a stylized Corinthian capital of the finest execution and the graffito of a *menorah* (seven-branched candlestick) which was drawn while the original golden candlestick was still standing in the Temple itself.

Of the tombs of the Herodian period several are of monumental proportions. One, the so-called 'Tomb of Absalom' in the Kidron

▷

Western (Wailing) Wall of the Herodian Temple enclosure, built of stone blocks with margin, 1 m. high. This section has been for centuries a place of prayer for the Jews, and of mourning for the destroyed temple.

Valley, is the monument of a tomb-cave (the 'Tomb of Jehoshaphat') behind it. The monument is partly rock-cut and partly built. It combines in the Oriental Hellenistic manner Ionic columns with a Doric frieze, and is surmounted by a conical pyramid, topped by a flower ornament. Another Herodian tomb is the 'Tomb of Herod's Family' near the King David Hotel; it has a rolling stone entrance, the stone used to close the entrance after a burial so as to keep it unviolated, and its walls are covered with stone slabs. The same method of covering the walls of an underground rock-cut cave can be observed in the 'Nazarite's Tomb' in the Hebrew University grounds on Mount Scopus. This area has yet another Herodian tomb, that of one Nicanor of Alexandria or of his family. He is mentioned in the Talmudic sources as the donor of the bronze doors of 'Nicanor's Gate' in the Temple.

Herodian enclosure wall around the traditional site of the Machpelah cave, where Abraham and his family were buried. The smooth base surmounted by a pilastered upper wall (the top is later) shows how the Temple wall once loocked.

Herod's interest in fortified places did not stop at Jerusalem. South-east of Bethlehem he built a fortress called 'Herodium', of circular shape, with four towers placed crosswise in the curtain wall. The fortress is provided with a bath, dwelling rooms, a banqueting hall and a synagogue. According to Josephus, Herod was buried here, but his tomb has not been discovered so far. The round fortress stands on a high, partly artificial, conical hill and was connected by an aqueduct with the rich springs of Ein Eitam on the Jerusalem-Hebron road.

The Herodian structures at Masada are still more impressive, because of the unique character of this fortress built on an isolated rock 300 m. above the Dead Sea. Herod regarded this place as a last refuge in case of need. The flat top of the rock is surrounded by a casemate wall with towers. Within the walls stands a big palace, with a throne

room and dwelling quarters, a guard room beside a monumental gate, and quarters for the palace workmen. Two other palace-like houses probably served the needs of the court. A large cistern cut in the top of the rock provided part of the water supply of Masada. A barracks structure stands north of the palace. Near the western gate of the fortress are the remains of a synagogue and of a pillared hall with benches around its walls, orientated towards Jerusalem. At the north end of the rock are storehouses consisting of long rooms placed side by side, an administrative building, and a large public bath of the hypocaust type, like Roman thermae. Smaller baths were provided within the palace. The pointed north end of the whole surface of the Masada rock is separated from the rest by a high wall with its own gate. It served as the private residence of the king, and is arranged in three tiers: a small dwelling house with a semi-circular platform in front of it stands on the topmost level. From there one descends to a round colonnaded *tholos* on the middle level; a further descent leads to the banqueting hall on the lowest level. Here Herod could feast and look down on humanity crawling below him in the plain. A few rooms, provided with private baths, are attached to the cliff wall still further down. The whole of the Herodian building complex was decorated with stuccoed columns having Corinthian or Ionian capitals in the Augustan style. The walls were painted to imitate marble, the floors paved with mosaics with geometric or floral ornaments. It is characteristic of this lonely fortress that even in his desert stronghold, Herod strictly observed the aniconic character of the Jewish law, as interpreted in his time. Masada is provided with an ingenious water system; two deep valleys supply its aqueducts with water flowing into two tiers of rock-cut cisterns below the fortress. As Josephus says, Masada was amply provided with food, arms and water for a garrison of a thousand men. Its fate was ultimately decided during the Jewish revolt.

Ruling over a non-Jewish area which formed about half of his kingdom, Herod took good care of the Greek cities of his realm. He rebuilt the town of Straton's Tower on the coast, and renamed it Caesarea. Adjoining the city he built a large harbour, which soon became the main port of Palestine. The city of Caesarea served for centuries as the capital of Palestine. Herodian remains are still to be seen, such as the harbour moles and vaults, the podium of the Temple of Augustus, a part of the Herodian wall and gate, the high-level aqueduct of the city, running northwards, and a theatre, which in its present form is post-Herodian but which still follows the original Herodian plan. The hippodrome can still be seen outside the city, with its sloping specta- tors' tiers and the porphyry obelisks which stood within it.

Another city restored by Herod was Samaria, which he called Sebaste (Sebastos = Augustus, in Greek). Here the city was provided with new walls and round tower gates; on the highest spot a temple of Augustus was built over the remains of the Israelite citadel; a

▷

Herodian monument, known as 'Absalom's Tomb'. The lower part is rock-cut with Ionian capitals and a Doric frieze. The upper part is built. The monument ends in a cylindrical pyramid crowned with a stone flower.

P. 60/61
Distant view of Herodium, fortress and burial place of King Herod.

Masada. Herodian magazines, excavated and restored.

◁
*The north end of Masada, showing the three palace terraces.
The 'Snake path' is on the left.*

Masada. Hypocaust room of the public bath.

monumental staircase leads up to it. A colonnaded street runs from the gate to the forum at the other end of the town.

Herod's ambivalent policy is evident also from his coinage. He revived some of the Hasmonaean symbols, such as the horns of plenty, and restored the pagan *caduceus* (symbol of Hermes) which was placed between them. On other coins he used the helmets of the Dioscuri surmounted by a star, or the *thymiaterion* or incense vessel used in the temples. On one coin he even had the eagle represented, although this symbol was a transgression of the Jewish law. It might have recalled the golden eagle which Herod had set up over the gate of the Temple, an act which led to a riot in Jerusalem.

The last years of Herod's reign were clouded by intrigues within his court, as a result of which he executed his two sons by the Hasmonaean Mariamme, killed by him some years previously. Almost with his last breath Herod ordered the execution of another son, Antipater. He left many splendid monuments, but died in 4 BC without having solved the main problem of his reign, the bridging of the gap between Judaism and the Graeco-Roman world.

Judaea after Herod

Herod did not regard any one of his three surviving sons as capable of ruling the whole of his kingdom. He suggested in his will that the kingdom should be divided between the three. After some hesitation, the emperor Augustus gave his approval and Herod's sons each received his share: Archelaus, Judaea and Samaria; Herod Antipas, Galilee and Peraea east of the Jordan; and Philip, the Gaulan, Batanaea and the Hauran. Within a decade Archelaus lost his kingdom and was replaced by a Roman procurator (governor). The procurators, originally fiscal officials, were chosen as a rule from among the lower paid grade of knights; while some of them were competent, many were cruel or corrupt.

The rule of the procurators was interrupted for a short time (41-44) in the reign of King Agrippa I. Although directly descended from Herod, the king found much more favour than his grandfather had by reason of his Jewish orthodoxy, which contrasted strangely with the adventurous life he had led before his enthronement. It is interesting to note that the Jewish sages supported Agrippa I even when he undertook measures which they would not have permitted to Herod. Thus Agrippa's coinage, issued in Jerusalem, was marked by a sunshade, symbol of royalty, and three barley-ears, and therefore unimpeachable from the orthodox point of view. In Caesarea, however, the same king struck coins not only with the image of the emperor but even with his own and that of his son. In Jerusalem, Agrippa I began the building of the Third Wall of the city on its northern side. This wall was completed after the outbreak of the First Revolt. Some of its remains are still visible not far from the Damascus Gate.

▷

Masada. Round structure on middle terrace of the three-tiered Herodian palace in the north. Roman camps and siege wall can be seen in the plain.

P. 66/67
Sebaste-Samaria. Herodian towers flanking city gate.

'Tomb of the Kings', Jerusalem. Monumental tomb of the first century AD. Court and entrance to tombs, with Doric frieze and foliate border below.

The reign of Agrippa has appeared to later generations as the Indian summer of the Second Temple period. During his time Jerusalem reached its greatest extent. Jewish spiritual activity was concentrated on the elaboration of the Oral law, the re-interpretation of the Mosaic Pentateuch in terms of the contemporary world. In the four generations after the death of Alexander Jannaeus, the spiritual leadership of the Jewish nation was in the hands of the Pharisees. At their head stood the 'Pairs' of Sages, beginning with Antigonus of Socho and ending with Hillel and Shammai in the time of Herod. They and their successors continued the work of the 'scribes' in the time of Ezra. Gradually an elaborate code of laws and regulations was evolved, which covered not only the purely religious duties of the devout Jews, but their family laws and the purity rituals connected with food. Those observing the Oral law were deemed 'trustworthy' and formed a voluntary organization of *haberim* ('associates') who could communicate with each other, while shunning the *am ha aretz* ('people of the land', i.e. the rest of the population). The latter, however, could be influenced by degrees to observe the Law, as interpreted by the leading Pharisees. The laws of ritual purity served also to separate Jews from Gentiles. Nevertheless there was much proselytizing activity in the Diaspora. The Jews who lived dispersed throughout the Roman empire and in Babylonia came in ever growing numbers to Jerusalem on pilgrimages;

'Tomb of the Kings', made for a royal family of Adiabene, Queen Helena and her children, the kings who adopted Judaism and settled in Jerusalem.

their contributions to the Temple and local charities became a highly important factor in the flourishing economy of the country.

The artistic trends of the period are marked as before by a strict interpretation of the Second Commandment. No human or animal figure appears on any of the thousand sarcophagi and ossuaries discovered so far. We can distinguish two trends at that time. One is based on Late Hellenistic and Oriental developments, parallels for which can be found in Palmyra and Nabatean reliefs, and is characterized by a rich ornamentation, based on the garland and the acanthus scroll, with a strong tendency to fill up all the available space (what is called a *horror vacui*). This rich style is especially evident in the sarcophagi found in the many tombs of wealthy people around Jerusalem. It is evident also in the floral ornament decorating the pediment of the so-called Tombs of the Judges in the Upper Kidron Valley, in the Tomb of the Grapes and in that of the Nazarite, also in the same vicinity. The most sumptuous of these funeral monuments is the Tomb of the Kings, just north of the Third Wall. It was made for a royal family of Adiabene (now in the vicinity of Mosul in Iraq), who had adopted Judaism and settled in Jerusalem. This tomb consists of a monumental staircase, a large rock-cut court, a façade in the Ionic style with a Doric frieze of triglyphs and metopes, enclosing shields. The frieze is broken by a symbolic representation of bunches of grapes flanked by wreaths. The whole is underlined by a leafy border strip in which various fruits are placed together on an acanthus background. The tomb proper is provided with a rolling stone. Inside, the burial chambers are arranged in several tiers. This monument, known as the Tomb of Queen Helena, who was mother of the kings of Adiabene, was once surmounted by three conical pyramids, and was a landmark in ancient Jerusalem.

Humbler burials were effected in ossuaries. Towards the end of the Second Temple period, belief in the resurrection of the individual, as propounded by the Pharisees, became general. It was associated with a distinction between the sinfulness of the flesh as contrasted with the permanence and incorruptibility of the skeleton. This belief was probably the origin of the custom of double burial, which was then introduced. The body was exposed for a year until the flesh was eaten away; then the skull and bones were carefully collected and interred in small rectangular stone boxes called ossuaries. About a thousand of these boxes have been discovered in various places in Judaea, but mainly around Jerusalem. Many of the ossuaries are not decorated, though a considerable proportion have ornaments, mostly geometric, incised with a knife. The most usual decoration consists of two rosettes within an ornamental frame. There are, however, many

General view of Nazareth.

cases of representations of buildings, flowers and objects, such as goblets or vases. These decorations may have symbolic meaning, but their precise interpretation still escapes us. In very many cases the names of the deceased were written on the ossuaries, in Hebrew, Aramaic or Greek, often with details of their profession. One such group, found recently in a tomb at Giveat Mivtar near Jerusalem, has become famous. Among the buried one man is described as 'Simeon, the builder of the Temple' (probably a stone mason to judge from his calloused bones). Another ossuary in this tomb contains the bones of a man who died by crucifixion. Often the bones of several individuals, up to four adults and children, were found in one ossuary. The ornamentation of these ossuaries is executed in a sharp geometrical style, based on a contrast between the well-lit, bright surface and the deep, dark background. The same lacelike effect is paralleled in the Parthian stucco façades found in Mesopotamian palaces in Hatra and Assur. It has been suggested that both are derived from the same Assyrian or Babylonian source. The Jews might have learned of this ornamental style during the Babylonian exile and brought it back with them on their return to Zion; since when it had become traditionally consecrated.

Jesus of Nazareth

The fall of the Hasmonaean kingdom and the loss of national independence caused a deep trauma among the Jewish people. As usual in times of stress, their thoughts turned to a future salvation, to Messianic hopes. The Messianic idea was first voiced in Judah by the prophet Isaiah as a consolation and a contrast to the story of woe which they foresaw in the immediate future as a punishment for the sins of the people. In the Babylonian exile it became connected with the Iranian idea of the coming end of this world, within cycles of destruction and rebirth of one world after another. The prophets of Israel did not stress this aspect of Messianism. For them the troubles which befell the Jewish people resulted from its sinfulness, its idolatry in particular, and the kings of Assyria and Babylonia were but the executors of the divine wrath. Having purged itself in exile, the nation could recover its spiritual integrity after the return to Zion. Its constancy was rewarded by the Hasmonaean revolt and freedom from foreign rule. The disasters which befell the Jewish people under the last Hasmonaeans could not be explained in this way, for there was now no idolatry in Israel. Clearly, the new troubles were the birthpangs of the Messianic era, now imminent. This understanding of contemporary history served as the background for the spiritual ferment of the times. The official Sadducees, the high priests and their following, did not share it. Their spiritual needs were fully met by the ritual of Temple worship. The Pharisees admitted the possibility of the approaching judgement. They solved the problem of individual salvation by trying to observe with ever-growing scrupulousness the rule of the Law, and to walk in a continually narrowing path of righteousness. The Zealots were ready to bring about the Messianic period by resorting to the short cut of an armed revolution. Against this background, various teachers, recorded in the history of the times, rose and led their followers towards a promised salvation but brought perdition upon them. It is in this context that the life and teaching of Jesus can be understood. Born at Bethlehem in the last year of Herod (probably December, 5 BC) Jesus was brought up in Nazareth. He was about thirty years of age when his brief ministry began. Baptized by John, probably near Jericho and the seat of the Qumran sect, Jesus might have absorbed something of the atmosphere of the Essenes, such as their community of means and 'love-feasts'. His main activity was, however, in the vicinity of the Sea of Galilee, in and around Capernaum, 'his city', Magdala, the home of Mary Magdalene, and Bethsaida whence came the apostles Peter, Andrew and Philip. After three years of preaching and wandering Jesus came to Jerusalem for the last time. There he was arrested, accused of blasphemy before the Sanhedrin, passed on to the Roman governor Pontius Pilate as a political criminal, condemned for rebellion and executed by the Romans by crucifixion.

This brief career on earth, which had worldwide historical repercussions, and which endowed the 'Land of Israel' with the status of a 'Holy Land' in the eyes of Christian millions, by its very nature left hardly any visible material trace.

For the early Christians the events related in the Gospels represented a unique intersection of the divine and the human spheres, localized both in time and space. Hence the geographical setting of

◁

Bethlehem. Nave of Church of the Nativity with Justinian's columns.

Bethlehem. Interior of Basilica of the Nativity seen through narthex.

Entrance to Grotto of the Nativity with Crusader pilasters (opposite, above).

Site of the Nativity inside the Grotto marked by a silver star.

the life of Jesus and of the apostles acquired for them a religious significance, expressed in the veneration of the 'holy sites' and in pilgrimages to them. As soon as possible (that is to say, from the fourth century onwards) these local traditions were given architectural expression in the shape of commemorative churches and chapels. As time proceeded these traditions were multiplied and sometimes split up between conflicting localities, especially after the schism between the

The Mount of Olives seen from Gethsemane.

Latin and Greek Orthodox churches. The insecurity which affected so much of the history of the Holy Land led to the creation of places of worship in the vicinity of the main roads, originally intended to commemorate inaccessible sanctuaries, but, in the course of time, supplanting them.

The Gospel story begins with the Annunciation, which has been identified with Nazareth and the grotto below the modern church.

Excavations have shown remains of houses of the Roman period in this area; the excavators have suggested that there is evidence of Judaeo-Christian worship there. The Nativity has been placed by the Gospels in a 'house' (*Matthew 2:11*) or a 'manger' (*Luke 2:7*) 'because there was no room for them in the inn'. From the middle of the second century tradition placed this event in a cave close to the village of Bethlehem in Judaea. From the time of Hadrian to that of Constantine the cave, with the grove about it, was dedicated to the worship of Thammuz-Adonis. In AD 326 the first Church of the Nativity, consisting of an octagon over the cave, adjoining a basilica, was built. It was replaced by Justinian with the Basilica of the Nativity as it stands at present, with a trefoil apse. Today the grotto is reached by a narrow staircase with Crusader portals and doors of bronze dating from the time of Justinian. The exact place of the Nativity is marked by a silver star in the grotto.

Jerusalem, Via Dolorosa. 5th Station, where, according to tradition, Simon of Cyrene took over the Cross carried by Jesus.

In Nazareth, another cave is known as the house and workshop of Joseph and Mary where Jesus grew up. This tradition cannot be verified. The 'well of Mary' has more substance, for it is the only spring in the village.

The site of the Baptism has been identified according to two different traditions. The more current one places it on the Jordan banks near Jericho; another tradition prefers a place south of Beth Shean. The sojourn of Jesus in the wilderness on a high mountain has been localized at the Byzantine monastery of Jebel Quruntul above Jericho, the site of the Maccabean fortress of Dok.

Most of Jesus's activity was concentrated around the Sea of Galilee. The locations of Capernaum and Chorazin (*Matthew 11:21*), as well as that of Magdala (*Mark 8:10,* in variant readings), are definite. The synagogue of Capernaum is, however, certainly not that in which Jesus taught. Recent excavations have, according to the claim of the

Via Dolorosa, 6th Station, where, according to tradition, St Veronica wiped the sweat off the face of Jesus.

excavators, uncovered nearby the 'House of Peter', which served as a place of worship for a Judaeo-Christian community in the second century and later. The mountain of the Beatitudes has been identified since Byzantine times with the site of the present modern church; the Miracle of the Loaves and Fishes was commemorated in the fifth century with the beautiful mosaics of the church at Heptapegon, below this mountain. The site of the miracle of Cana is placed at Kafr Kanna near Nazareth, although many scholars would prefer to locate it at Khirbet Kana, higher up the mountains, near Jotapata. The drowning of the Gadarene swine took place, according to some, near Zemach, while others place it at Gergesa (Kursi) on the eastern shore of the lake, where a Byzantine church and monastery have recently been discovered. The rocky cliff of Paneas (Caesarea Philippi) might have inspired the comparison of Peter to 'the rock' on which the church was to be built (*Matthew 16:18,* etc.). From Byzantine times the 'high mountain' of the Transfiguration (*Mark 9:2*) has been identified with Mount Tabor, and a church built to commemorate the event. The talk with the Samaritan woman is connected in the Gospels with the 'well of Jacob' near Sychar. This site has been commemorated in Byzantine times by a cruciform church near Askar, in the vicinity of Nablus.

The last days of Jesus in Jerusalem and its neighbourhood have received the attention of topographers in proportion to the outstanding importance of the Crucifixion in Christian theology. The difficulty of locating the many places mentioned in the Gospel story lies in the fact that the Old City of Jerusalem, built in the shape established by the Roman colony of Aelia, differs greatly from the ancient town of Herod and the procurators, quite apart from the fact that the street level has, in the last nineteen centuries, risen by 25 m. in some places. The location of the Mount of Olives is, of course, certain, and so is that of the Temple. The Last Supper is commemorated by the Crusader hall of the Coenaculum on 'Mount Zion', near the 'House of Caiphas'. Apart from the fact that the house of the high-priest was certainly in the Upper City, these locations are based on tradition only. The location of the Lithostrotos on which Pilate judged Jesus is subject to dispute. The traditional site is in the ruins of the Antonia, on the pavement in the crypt of the convent of Our Lady of Zion, near the 'Ecce Homo' arch, which is certainly of a later date. Other scholars, including some Catholics, place the judgment at Herod's palace near the Jaffa Gate. Only by following the first assumption can the Via Dolorosa, as it now exists, reproduce even a trace of the Way of the Cross. The detailed placing of the various stations, the Flagellation, the Spasm of the Virgin, the place where Simon of Cyrene took over the Cross, the place where St Veronica dried the face of Jesus, dates from the Crusader period. The site of Golgotha and of the Holy Sepulchre had been in Roman times under the Temple of Aphrodite adjoining the Forum of Aelia Capitolina. There was some doubt about its exact location, although its general position must have been known to the Christian community which continued to live in Jerusalem after 135. The miracle of the finding of the True Cross put an end to such doubts. The Constantinian basilica was built in place of the pagan temple and its western part has been located in the Russian

▷

Roman and Byzantine remains round the pool of Bethesda (Sheep's Pool) where the miraculous healing (John 5) is traditionally located. The deep pool is rock cut; it consisted of two basins separated by a dam.

Landscape of Judaean desert where Jesus retired after baptism on the River Jordan.

monastery near the Holy Sepulchre and its apse has recently been excavated under the 'Catholicon' of the church itself. The present rotunda surrounding the aedicule of the Holy Sepulchre still stands on a Constantinian base. The rock of Golgotha, which was cut into the shape of a cube by Constantine's architects, now bears the Crusader chapel of the Calvary. The Holy Sepulchre consisted of a stone surface, now covered by a marble slab and housed within a construction erected about 1810. The body of the church is of Crusader construction, the crypt of St Helena is Byzantine, with later additions. The authenticity of the site naturally depends on the line of the second wall of Herodian

Jerusalem; in any case the so-called 'Garden Tomb' outside Damascus Gate is dismissed by most scholars as apocryphal. The site of the Ascension on the Mount of Olives was commemorated in Byzantine times by an octagonal church, most of which is still standing. The foundations of the Byzantine and Crusader churches below the present church at Gethsemane show that, at least since the fourth century, this had been the site venerated as the place of the arrest and agony of Jesus. Two holy sites in Jerusalem are connected in particular with the Virgin Mary: the place of her 'Dormition' on Mount Zion, where a modern church commemorates the event, and

her Tomb in the Kidron Valley. At Bethany (el Azariye), east of
Jerusalem, a Byzantine church commemorated the site of the house
of Mary and Martha and the tomb of Lazarus. It was preceded on
the site by Jewish tombs of the first century.

Since Byzantine times active promotion has endowed more and
more sites and monuments with a temporary holiness, often transferred from one place to another in the interests of easier acces-
sibility. Scientific, historical, topographical and archaeological research
has disproved many of the so-called 'holy sites', which nevertheless
remain consecrated at the metaphysical and spiritual level by the
piety lavished on them for centuries. Research has, however, also
provided concrete evidence or parallels here and there for the details

*General view of 'Mount Zion', Jerusalem. In the centre the Church of the
Dormition of the Virgin Mary can be seen; to the right stands the
Coenaculum, the traditional site of the Last Supper. Below it, the 'Tomb
of David' which has been venerated since the Middle Ages or even earlier.*

of the Gospel story. Thus we can now see the name of Pontius Pilate engraved on a stone, part of the dedication of a Tiberieum at Caesarea and found re-used in the theatre there. Coins such as Jesus used to demonstrate what was due to Caesar (*Matthew 22:19-21*) are still preserved, as is the 'widow's mite' (*Mark 12:41*). The huge walls of the Temple enclosure make us understand how the disciples marvelled when Jesus foretold the destruction of the Sanctuary (*Mark 13:2*). The 'seat of Moses', a chair of honour in the synagogues, has been found in the Chorazin synagogue (*Matthew 23:2*); 'rolling stones' (*Matthew 27:60*) exist at the Tomb of the Kings and the Herodian monument at Jerusalem. An inscription from the 'Synagogue of the Libertines' (*Acts 6:9*) has been found on the Ophel hill, Jerusalem. It records

P. 86/87
*The traditional site of the Garden of Gethsemane with
the eastern wall of Jerusalem above.*

one Theodotus son of Vettenius, i.e. a freedman of the Vetii family. Most people, however, will discover the atmosphere of the time of Jesus in the landscapes of the Holy Land: the blue waters of the Sea of Galilee are still by turns stormy and tranquil, the fertile plain of Gennesaret still stretches out beside the lake named after it, the hills of Nazareth are as they were at the time of Jesus and so are the Mount of Olives and the desert of Judah—in fact, because of its desolate character, it is even nearer to its pristine state. The climate of Palestine has not changed appreciably, even if so many other things have altered on the social and political scene.

The Destruction of Jerusalem and Judaea in the First and Second Revolts against Rome

Messianic fervour and Roman misrule finally drove the majority of the Jews of Palestine to two successive revolts against the ruling power. The traumatic shock of the mad emperor Caligula's order to have his statue set up in the Temple shook belief in Roman religious tolerance and provided a misleading historical analogy with the Hasmonaean uprising.

The revolt broke out in AD 66, at Masada on the shores of the Dead Sea. The insurgents seized Jerusalem and evicted the Roman garrisons from Herod's towers and from the Antonia. They quickly secured possession of all Judaea and Galilee. It took the Roman general Vespasian (the future emperor) and his son Titus three years to suppress the revolt, first in Galilee and then in Judaea. The main revolt ended with the siege of Jerusalem (April-August 70) and the destruction of the Temple and most of the city. The last stronghold of the zealots, Masada, fell after a dramatic siege in 74.

Recent excavations have provided ample evidence of the destruction wrought in these battles and sieges. In Jerusalem, excavations along the southern wall of the Temple esplanade have led to the discovery of huge blocks of masonry which crashed down in the year 70 to the Herodian street, 30 m. and more below, smashing the pavement slabs in the process. Another vivid illustration of the general destruction wrought in Jerusalem at this time has been uncovered in the Jewish Quarter of the Old City, the Upper City of Herodian times. There the foundations of a house were found, undisturbed since the siege of Titus. The substructures which served as kitchens and cellars are complete with their marble tables, pottery, weights and measures, emplacements for ovens and so forth. There is even a spear standing in a corner all ready for use although is does not seem to have been of much help. A seal found in the ruins gives the name of the owner of the house, Bar Kathros, a family identified in Talmudic sources. The whole area was burned red and black through a huge conflagration which must have raged when the Romans captured it.

Jerusalem has been inhabited continuously since AD 70, and most of the evidence of Titus's siege and destruction has long ago been covered over by the houses of the living. There is, however, one site which has remained almost untouched since the First Revolt, and that is Masada. We have seen how Herod transformed a lonely rock into a magnificent palace-fortress. Excavations have supplied the record of

◁
Interior of the Holy Sepulchre.

the next chapter in the story of this stronghold. Occupied by the Zealots at the very beginning of the revolt, it remained in their hands for at least eight years, according to ample evidence. The Zealots settled in the Herodian palaces and casemate walls, subdividing them, allotting areas for their own domestic or administrative purposes, and leaving their mark everywhere. The synagogue was rebuilt, providing a separate small room for the sacred texts. Ritual baths enabled the warriors to observe the law of purity. Various graffiti on sherds, or written *ostraca,* provide evidence of the distribution of food and other needs. One of the sherds bears the name of the commander of Masada, Ben Yair. The excavators found part of the text of *Ecclesiasticus* (Ben Sira), documents of the Dead Sea sect, phylacteries, etc. Looking down from Masada on to the plain below one can see the whole outline of the Roman order of battle: two big camps for half a legion each, one on the eastern side, another on the western higher up the cliff, with six supplementary camps for the auxiliaries. Each of the eight camps has a stone wall round it and a uniform distribution of functional and dwelling inner structures. Between the camps runs the *circumvallatio,* a stone wall encircling the fortress on every side except for some of the quite inaccessible cliffs to the south. This served to cut off Masada from all outside succour and to keep the besieged confined within their eyrie. Here and there the wall around the fortress grows wider: these are the places where engines of war, catapults or ballistae, were stationed. On the western side of the fortress is visible the 'White rock' (*Leuke*) from which point the Romans began building their siege dam (*agger*). The foundations of the dam are still in evidence as they rise up to the fortress. It was on this dam that the Romans rolled up their siege tower, which was provided with a battering ram. As soon as they reached the fortress wall, Masada was doomed. The besieged in their extremity set up a wooden wall beyond the breach made by the iron ram within the tower. The Romans tried to set it on fire but, for a time, the wind blew in their direction, away from the new wall. Then the wind changed and the wall was consumed. Sure of victory, the Romans retreated for the night. During that pause in the fighting the leader of the Zealots, Eleazar the son of Yair, succeeded in persuading the defenders to kill their wives and children and to commit suicide, so as not to become slaves of the Romans. This was accomplished, and in the morning the Romans found only the dead bodies of the garrison. In the excavations of Masada various skeletons of both men and women have been found, attesting to the truth of this tragic story.

After sixty-two years of an uneasy truce the Second Revolt broke out in 132, in the time of the emperor Hadrian. Its primary cause was the emperor's decision to set up a Roman colony on the site of Jerusalem. It was to be called Aelia Capitolina. The usual foundation ceremonies were performed, including the driving of a plough around its planned periphery. This act of the governor Tineius Rufus appeared in Jewish eyes as an unspeakable blasphemy. The revolt which broke out is also known as the War of Bar Kokhba, after the name of its great leader. Simeon Bar Kosiba, as he was really called (the name Bar Kokhba, 'Son of the Star', refers to his Messianic claims), succeeded in forcing the Romans to evacuate Jerusalem and was able to set up a regular government which began a new era ('of the Freedom of Israel'), and had its own coinage, tribunals and land registries. After three years the Romans succeeded, by using seven legions, in locking up Bar Kokhba

Old olive trees in the Garden of Gethsemane.

in the fortress of Beth Ther, south-west of Jerusalem, and destroying him there.

The story of the Bar Kokhba revolt has now been vividly brought to life by discoveries in caves bordering the deep rift valleys near the Dead Sea. In Wadi Murabbaat and in Nahal Hever documents and other remains were found in caves which served as refuges from the Romans for the remaining rebels. Several such caves have been found, with Roman camps sited on the top of the cliffs. The Romans could not storm the inaccessible caves and set out to starve the besieged. In some cases, as in the 'Cave of Horrors', there seems to have been first slow starvation, then a bonfire of all goods and a mass suicide. Others in the same predicament may have surrendered or escaped. One of the caves, the 'Cave of Letters', served as a refuge for the commanders of Engeddi under Bar Kokhba. They took with them their official archives, including several letters issued by 'Simeon Bar Kosiba, Prince of Israel', but written of course by a scribe. These letters, in Hebrew, Aramaic and Greek, inform us of the difficulties of the revolutionary government as regards supplies, the treatment of prisoners and the observance of religious practices. The archives also included leases and other private documents, in particular those of one Babatha, a female

P. 92/93
Masada. View of Roman siege wall and camps.

The northern gate and part of the central opening of the 'Ecce Homo' arch,
a triumphal gate of Roman Jerusalem (Aelia Capitolina).
Now in the Church of the Convent of Notre Dame de Sion.

relation of one of the commanders. They allow us to follow almost
the whole life of this propertied woman, her marriages, her law-
suits and their results. The cave also contained a wealth of objects
of daily use: baskets, wool ready for weaving, clothes, cosmetics, uten-
sils, a multitude of keys of all sizes—apparently the heads of families
had locked up their houses and taken the keys with them, hoping for
a speedy return which never materialized. Most interesting are the
remains of booty taken from some Roman regiment: a set of sacrificial

bowls and jugs, some of them once ornamented with representations of mythological personages. Whenever they could, the warriors of Bar Kokhba slashed these offending images with deep strokes of their knives. The booty also included beautiful moulded and cut glass, carefully wrapped in palm leaves.

After the revolt the emperor Hadrian ordered the expulsion of all the 'circumcised' from the area of Aelia Capitolina; even the Judaeo-Christians had to leave. In their place he settled Syrians and Arabians. The name of Judaea was changed to Syria-Palaestina (hence our 'Palestine'). With the close of the era of revolts, a new reality began in the Holy Land, with the Jews confined largely to Galilee and the rest of the country reverting to paganism.

Roman Palestine

Almost two centuries elapsed between the end of the Bar Kokhba war and the passing of Palestine into the hands of Constantine, the first Christian emperor. The years from 135 to 324 are among the most tranquil in the history of the Holy Land. The Jews, defeated and confined mainly to Galilee, turned their energies inwards and developed both the Oral Law and their religious art. The province, one of the smallest in the Roman empire, was garrisoned by two legions, the Tenth Fretensis at Jerusalem and the Sixth Ferrata ('Ironsides') at Legio (Lajjun) in the Valley of Jezreel. Sharing in the political and economic vicissitudes of the empire, Palestine was also part of the uniform culture of the Roman world. Almost the whole of its area was divided into municipal territories, for the Romans had inherited from the Greeks the belief that only city life was fit for civilized man. The cities were provided with the amenities of a Roman colony: temples for the gods, offices for the administration, broad streets crossing at right angles (with the main thoroughfares colonnaded), theatres and hippodromes for entertainment, public baths fed by long aqueducts for cleanliness, walls and gates for security. Although the peace was occasionally disturbed by a civil war or a Bedouin raid, and although the country suffered, together with the rest of the empire, from a grievous economic crisis in the third century, on the whole it was a period of quiet material development.

Situated in the eastern part of the Roman empire, the dominant culture of Palestine in this epoch was Greek. The only signs of the domination of a Latin race are the Latin inscriptions (dedications, epitaphs, milestones), mostly connected with the emperors and the army. Remains of Roman roads and bridges found all over the country, together with hundreds of milestones giving the titles and names of the emperors who paved or repaired the roads, attest to the importance of communications in the eyes of the imperial government. It has been noticed that the road repairs became especially numerous before every war with the Parthians who dwelt towards the East. The Romans began by paving the coastal road from Acre to Gaza, connecting it with Antioch in the north and Pelusium in Egypt; then they connected Caesarea with Jerusalem, so that their governor might have easy communications with the legion he commanded. The establishment of a legionary camp at Legio required another set of radiating roads to Caesarea and into Galilee. The foundation of Aelia at Jerusalem made equally necessary roads to Ascalon and Gaza to the west, and Jericho to the east.

The remains of Aelia itself are not numerous. The so-called 'Ecce Homo' arch is a Roman triumphal monument set up by the colony.

Some remains of an aedicule of the Temple of Venus have been found below the Holy Sepulchre. The towers near Damascus gate, and the gate between them, were rebuilt at a time when the colony was provided with a wall because of increasing insecurity in the third century. There are a few Latin inscriptions dedicated to the emperors from Antoninus Pius to Septimius Severus. But the most lasting monument to Roman orderliness is, paradoxically, the Old City of Jerusalem. For all its crooked and narrow lanes, the basic plan of this quarter is still that of a Roman camp, with local modifications. It is almost a square (or rhomb) intersected by a cardo and decamus. The former had been split into two for reasons of local topography.

Jerusalem had been provided with an aqueduct in the last stage of the Second Temple, on a line 70 km. long from the vicinity of Hebron. It gained a second aqueduct leading from the so-called 'Pools of Solomon', near Ein Etam in the south, probably in the days of Septimus Severus.

Of the other great Roman cities, Ascalon still contains the remains of a council hall of semi-circular shape with a portico attached; although originally set up by Herod, the building had been extensively remodelled by the time of Septimius Severus. The sculptures are typically late Roman and include reliefs of Atlas carrying the celestial globe, surmounted by a winged victory—symbols of the divine favour vouchsafed to the imperial house—and a figure of Isis with her son Harpocrates. This and a set of figurines of Egyptian gods also found at Ascalon are evidence of the strong attraction which the culture of the Nile Valley still exerted in southern Palestine long after the Pharaohs had lain in the dust.

Remains from the time of Trajan have also been found at Jaffa. The city remained inhabited by Jews, and the weights issued by a Jewish market official (the *agoranomos*) have been found in the excavations.

Caesarea-by-the-sea remained the greatest Roman city, the capital of the province and its principal harbour. The huge site has only been very partially excavated, but even so its ruins are imposing. Besides many works of art (such as the statue of the dancing Satyr) and inscriptions, the city still displays a theatre of Herodian origin, reconstructed in Roman times. The seat of the governor is still visible. The theatre has many interesting features such as a painted pavement in the orchestra, which was renewed every year for fourteen years. The superimposed layers of geometric ornament have been studied by the excavators one after another.

The aqueduct of Caesarea is the most imposing monument of utilitarian architecture extant in this country. Originally it was probably the work of Herod. Later Caesarea had a second aqueduct. The high-level one brought water from high up in the Carmel range. After crossing the coastal plain on low spans it cuts across a hilly ridge by tunnel and turns southwards towards the city on high arches which are still standing. Another aqueduct was built in the time of Hadrian. Remains of inscriptions of the legionary detachments who worked on its extension and repair are still visible. This second (low-level)

▷

Ascalon. General view of ruins of Roman council hall and portico.

P. 98/99

Solomon's Pools near Bethlehem, part of Roman aqueduct of Aelia Capitolina.

Ascalon. 3rd-century reliefs from Council Hall. (Right) Victory holding a palm branch, standing on the celestial globe, supported by a crouching Atlas.

(Far right) Isis and Harpocrates.

aqueduct brought water for irrigation from the north, on its way crossing the Taninim (Zerqa) river on arches.

Under the governor Pontius Pilate, several important temples were built in Caesarea, one dedicated to Tiberius, another to Hadrian, the Hadrianeum. A porphyry statue of Hadrian, now reduced to a torso, but still weighing seven tons, was later set up by a Byzantine mayor of Caesarea in a public square of the city. It can be seen as it was found by the excavators, with another statue (or rather the combined fragments of two statues) representing Zeus, made of white marble, which is set up on a pedestal facing the torso of Hadrian.

Further inland the city of Sebaste (once Samaria) was another Roman colony. Although less resplendent than Caesarea, it shows many of the typical features of a Roman provincial city. Septimius Severus, who favoured Sebaste, provided it with a forum and an adjacent basilica, the columns of which have remained standing above ground throughout the ages. The Temple of Augustus, built by Herod, was reshaped. A colonnaded street connected the western city gate with the forum; on it stood a small temple of Kore, with a statue of the goddess and an inscription proclaiming: 'God is One; great is Kore the Unvanquished.' The neighbouring city of Neapolis is now submerged by Arabic Nablus, but on the sacred mountain of the Samaritans, Mount Gerizim, south of the city, are the remains of a temple of Zeus built in Roman times. It stands at the head of a staircase of a thousand steps. Both temple and staircase are reproduced on Roman coins.

Beth Shean (Scythopolis) was also a Roman town of importance. It

boasts perhaps the best-preserved Roman theatre west of the Jordan. The statues of pagan gods were removed in Christian times; that of a young god or hero, hidden away in a trench, was found when the theatre was excavated a few years ago. The theatre was exceptionally well equipped, with towers flanking the stage, from which the machinery of flying gods and heroes could be manipulated.

Near the spot where the Jordan river leaves the Sea of Galilee is an important site called Beth Yerah (in Greek, Philoteria, after a sister of Ptolemy I). We have already had occasion to mention it in connection with its Early Bronze remains. Immediately adjoining the Canaanite silo are a Roman fortress of rectangular shape and a Roman bath. The latter, which was supplied with water from the aqueduct of Tiberias by means of a subsidiary outlet, is a well-preserved example of a Roman country bath. It has a cool room (*frigidarium*) with a pool in the centre and benches around the walls. The marks of the marble pavement, as well as of the half-screen round the pool, can still be seen. The tepid and warm rooms formed one L-shaped hall, heated by hot air from beneath the floor which rested on small brick columns. There are two marble bath-tubs set in the thick walls of the hall. A furnace, with a store-room for wood, completed the installation.

P. 102/103
Caesarea, Mole of Herod's harbour re-used in Crusader times, with drums of Roman columns taken to strengthen walling.

101

Even Tiberias, although the centre of Jewish Galilee, was provided with a bath, remains of which have been excavated.

The northernmost Roman ruin of Palestine, which stands in lonely splendour, is the temple at Kadesh (Kadasa). It had a high portal ornamented with reliefs, including the winged sundisk. Roman tombs found in various sites include a mausoleum near the village of Mazor (the so-called Maqam en-Nabi Yahya). This is the only building dating from the Roman period which still carries its roof. The sarcophagi which adorned the Roman tombs were decorated with scenes from mythology or with symbolical ornaments. They include a pair of coffins found near Caesarea, one with an Amazonomachy, and the sarcophagus of the Seasons and Dionysos, found in the village of Turmus Aiya and now in the Jerusalem Citadel.

From the Hellenistic period onwards, the Orient contained two superimposed cultures: the official Graeco-Roman culture, based on the Greek language, the Olympian religion, and the literature, mythology and art of classical Greece as modified in the Hellenistic age; and a sub-culture of Oriental character, with an ambivalent relationship to the official culture: part struggle and part adaptation. The Orientals kept the essence of their religion and national traditions (in fact they even passed some of them on to the dominant Greeks and Romans). At the same time they adapted the exterior forms of Greeks art to their ornamental or ritual needs.

One of these Oriental sub-cultures was the Jewish one, flourishing in Roman Palestine. After the War of Bar Kokhba and the disaster in which it ended came a short but savage period of persecution and repression, directed by Hadrian against the surviving Jews. When this failed in face of the proverbial stubbornness of the Jewish nation, a 'stiff-necked' people if there ever was one, the emperor Antoninus Pius adopted a policy of appeasement. He permitted Judaism to exist as a lawful religion (*religio licita*), with its own institutions, although he accepted no compromise as regards Jerusalem and proselytizing. The Romans allowed the Jews to regain control of the municipalities in the Jewish towns, to reassemble the Sanhedrin with the Patriarch from the house of Hillel at its head, to set up their own courts (thinly disguised as courts of arbitration), and in general to pursue their activities undisturbed, as long as peace was kept and the taxes were paid. Sobered by the disasters of two lost revolts, the Jews acquiesced in Roman rule, bearing it as a 'punishment from heaven'. They were consoled to a certain extent by the splendour and power of their patriarchs, in particular Rabbi Judah I, the friend of emperors and the codifier of the Oral Law, the Mishnah. Having been deprived of their national centre, the Temple, the Jews turned with growing intensity towards the hundreds of synagogues in towns and villages, each becoming a place of study for the development of the Oral Law, the 'Jewish way of life' of those days.

During this period of appeasement and consolidation, a change of attitude is noticeable among the Jews towards the Graeco-Roman art, and in particular towards the representation of men and beasts. As has been noted, these were strictly forbidden in the time of the Second Temple and even down to the period of Bar Kokhba. Such representations

◁
Caesarea high-level aqueduct. Built in the first century BC *or* AD *by Herod or by the first procurators, repaired by Roman soldiers in the time of Hadrian. The water came from the Carmel range at a distance of 12 km.*

were regarded as being contrary to the Second Commandment: 'Thou shalt not make unto thee any graven images or any likeness of anything that is in heaven above', which command was interpreted strictly and literally. Later on rabbinical opinion changed: the aim of the commandment was to prevent idolatry, as was clear from its context: 'Thou shalt not bow down thyself to them'; hence images not tainted with worship of idols could be tolerated. A line was drawn against three-dimensional sculpture, which came uncomfortably close to imitating the work of the Creator. But as regards reliefs and paintings, there was much more permissiveness than heretofore. The decline in the belief in the Olympic gods, which was general in the third century, might have had something to do with this rabbinical liberalism. There was now obviously much less danger of idolatry. A typical anecdote of the

Caesarea. Open space made by 6th-century mayor, Flavius Strategius, who re-used statues from Roman temples to decorate it.

period tells how the Patriarch Gamaliel quietly went on using the bath of Aphrodite at Acre, even after he had been shown a statue of the goddess adorning it—he regarded it as a decoration, not an object of worship. The increased self-confidence of the Jewish leaders, based on the achievement of a codified Oral Law, might also have influenced them. In any case human and animal representations, and even mythological scenes, now appear in the decoration of Jewish synagogues and tombs.

The Galilean synagogues of the third and fourth centuries belong to what is called the 'early' class. They are basilical buildings, square or rectangular, marked with two parallel rows of columns lengthwise and one row across the width. These synagogues are plain inside, with benches running along their sides. They have no permanent place for

Caesarea. 3rd-century sarcophagus representing an Amazonomachy. Attic marble and workmanship. The unfinished head would seem to indicate that such sarcophagi were ready-made for an eventual order. Rockefeller Museum.

the Scrolls of the Law which are an integral part of the synagogue service. The scrolls were probably brought in from an adjacent store room. The upper part of the synagogue's interior was surrounded by a women's gallery adorned with a decorative frieze in relief. The main decorative features were on the façade, which was turned towards the Holy City and had three doors, the central one higher and wider than the other two. Over the doors were windows in ornate frames and above them the so-called Syrian pediment with the usual triangular shape, but now varied by a curved base.

This kind of building is found in Galilee at Capernaum, Meron, Kefar Bar'am, Chorazin and several other sites. Although the architectural planning, the orders and the basic ornament were borrowed by the builders from the current style of Roman architecture in Syria, the special features (the orientation in the direction of Jerusalem and the interior arrangements) were original developments. The architects had to provide a place of worship which constituted a new challenge in the history of religious architecture. Hitherto all temples (that of Jerusalem included) were regarded as the abode of the deity, immanent in the spirit or—in pagan temples—in the sacred statue. The sanctuary was therefore set apart for the priests. Its most sacred part, the holy of holies, was almost inaccessible. The mass of the worshippers assembled in the courtyard of the temple around an altar standing under heaven. With the destruction of the Temple, Jewish worship

◁
Caesarea. Statue of Artemis found near the theatre. Israel Museum.

Sebaste. Roman theatre.

abandoned sacrifice; the prayers were combined with the teaching of the Law, both obligatory on all members of the congregation. As a result, a functional building had to be provided which could hold many people, which was well lit (so as to make possible the reading of the Law), and in which there was nothing to distract the attention of the worshippers from their spiritual task. On the other hand the outside of the building was to represent with dignity the power of God and the devotion of the community; it was ornamented as richly as possible.

When the synagogal ornament of the early period was first studied by Kohl and Watzinger in 1904-5, its 'pagan' character caused these scholars to believe that the synagogues were designed and erected by Gentile architects and builders, and were presented by Roman emperors to the Jews, who had to accept the Danaean gift, even if unwillingly. Another theory, now disproved, was advanced by E.R. Goodenough; he saw in this Jewish art of the third century signs of an unorthodox, 'mystical' Judaism, opposed to the rabbinical establishment. As we shall see, the finds at Beth Shearim completely demolished both theories.

In fact the decoration of some of the synagogues, in particular that of Chorazin, but to some extent also that of Capernaum, is astonishing if we compare it with the ornamentation of the Jewish tombs in Jerusalem. Besides some clearly Jewish symbols, such as the seven-branched candlestick (*menorah*), which by this time had become the general symbol of Judaism, or the Ark of the Covenant (an aedicule with a gable, which was used to keep the Scrolls of the Torah), or the Tabernacle (a box with a rounded roof, on wheels), we find general magic symbols, such as the pentagram ('The Seal of Solomon') or the hexagram, which, as the 'Shield of David', at a much later stage became another symbol of Judaism. But we also find elements derived from the lower reaches of paganism: griffins, the Medusa head, the solar eagle holding garlands. It is astonishing to see how the eagle, which when set up by Herod over the gate of the Temple caused a bloody riot, was generally set over synagogue lintels only a couple of centuries later. Other ornaments showed centaurs, Hercules, or Nike bearing the palm-branch of Victory. Scenes of daily life, such as grape-harvesting, also occurred. All these representations, although by themselves not involving the great gods of the pagan pantheon, required the use of figurative art. Of sculpture in the round there was none, except the symbolical figures of lions.

The discovery of the big Jewish necropolis at Beth Shearim (excavated from 1936 onwards by B. Mazar and N. Avigad) caused a revolution in our view of Jewish art. This small Galilean township became famous as the seat of the great Patriarch Judah I and of his Sanhedrin. When the patriarch died at Sepphoris, he was brought to be buried in 'his' Beth Shearim (his tomb and that of his sons were discovered in catacomb No. 14). From the third century onwards, Beth Shearim became a central burial place for Jews from as far away as Palmyra, Beirut, Sidon, etc. The dead were interred in extensive catacombs, over thirty of which have been excavated. Each catacomb consisted of an entrance

▷
Aerial view of Capernaum.
Synagogue and vicinity. In foreground, remains of a
Byzantine church, below which stood, according to excavators,
the House of St Peter, venerated from the second century onward.
Behind, the synagogue with hall on left and court on right.

◁
*Capernaum synagogue. 3rd-century
interior, with restored north
wall and colonnade.*

*Above, details of frieze with floral
ornament, rosettes and magic signs.*

P. 116/117
*Meiron synagogue. Remains of
façade with three entrances,
right one restored.*

hall and burial chambers with *arcosolia* (arched-over burial troughs), or *loculi* (rectangular spaces cut into the rock). In one case (catacomb No. 11) the underground burial place was surmounted by a mausoleum; two of the catacombs (Nos. 14 and 20) have ornate arched façades

Kefar Bar'am synagogue. View of façade with three entrances. Relieving arch over middle door. Windows over side doors. Portico in front of façade still partly standing. 3rd century.

and above them open-air places for prayer orientated towards Jerusalem. The decoration of the mausoleum over No. 11 includes a mosaic pavement with representations of dolphins and an arched frieze with the eagle in the centre of the arch; on one side there is a peaceful procession

of animals, while on the other some wolves are tearing each other to pieces. Inside the mausoleum was a sarcophagus (apparently re-used) with the myths of Achilles on Scyros and of Meleager on its long sides, and of Leda and the swan on its short side. The accompanying inscription is in Greek.

While one could shrug off this use of pagan mythology in a Jewish cemetery as a symbol of the Hellenization of the Jewish Diaspora, catacomb No. 20 upset these preconceived views. Its inscriptions, in Hebrew this time, refer to the 'holy rabbis' and to a relative of a patriarch buried there. Nevertheless fragments of sarcophagi with Greek myths (such as an Amazonomachy) were found in this catacomb, together with stone coffins, obviously of local make, on which are depicted a hunter and his dog, lions, a human bearded mask, eagles, bulls, etc. Obviously, therefore, the official Jewish art of the third and early fourth centuries did allow such representations—a view which is supported by some passages in the Talmud.

Stylistically, such examples of Jewish art as have survived represent the usual Eastern blend of provincial art: a strong formal adherence to the patterns of Hellenistic-Roman art, combined with a continuance of Oriental traditions in the execution. We find many examples of the stylization of design in representations both of animals and of plants: the use of optic—as distinguished from plastic—values resorted to sharply contrasted light and shade. The cutting of the planes recalls similar decorations on Jewish ossuaries of the Second Temple period already discussed. In the representations of human beings there is a strong tendency to frontality (all figures face the viewer) and to isocephaly (all heads are at one level). The elements of Orientalizing Jewish art, discovered in the Dura-Europos synagogue, can be also traced at Beth Shearim and in the Galilean synagogues.

In the fourth century changes began to be made in the synagogue plan in order to obviate the inconvenience of a façade with doors turned towards Jerusalem. This arrangement obliged the worshippers either to use a side door, leaving the main portals for ornamental use only, or to make a right-about-turn after entering. In some Galilean synagogues, and in those of southern Judaea (where a few communities survived the Hadrianic decree of expulsion), a type of 'broad house' synagogue evolved, with a long wall facing Jerusalem, and doors in the short side. A niche for the Ark of the Covenant, flanked by two smaller ones for two seven-branched candlesticks, is provided in the wall facing Jerusalem. The worshippers entered by a door on the short side and turned their faces to the Holy City. These southern synagogues, at Eshthemoa and Susiya, are paved with mosaics (all the earlier Galilean synagogues had stone pavements). We are not yet able to determine whether these pavements belonged to the original buildings or were constructed later.

In 324 the history of Palestine was transformed by the victory of Constantine, a declared Christian, over his rival Licinius at Chalcedon. The Roman period ended and the Byzantine began in that year.

◁

Kefar Barʿam synagogue. View of interior row of columns through right-hand door.

P. 122/123

Beth Shearim. Catacomb No. 20. Inside of tomb cave with ornamented coffins.

Beth Shearim. 3rd-4th century-Jewish necropolis. Façade of Catacomb No. 20 with triple entrance, each door arched over.

Hammath-Tiberias. Seven-branched candlestick from synagogue, ornamented with 'knops and flowers'. 4th century. Israel Museum.

Griffon with wheel symbolizing Nemesis, the divine justice. 3rd century. Found at Erez near Ascalon. Israel Museum (below, left).

Limestone plaque for suspension with seven-branched candlestick, flanking an apotropaic mirror, intended to cast back an 'evil eye'. Gabled roof, with round arch and 'windows' below. 4th-5th century. Israel Museum.

The Byzantine Period (324-640)

The accession of a Christian emperor completely changed the status of Palestine. From a small province of the empire, of no particular importance to the government, it became the Holy Land of a widespread religion, propagated by the emperor himself. Immediately after the council of Nicaea (325), Constantine and his mother Helena began to transform Jerusalem into a Christian city. The empress visited Jerusalem and during her stay the miracle of the Finding of the True Cross occurred. Constantine decided to erect a splendid church over the site, below the temple of Venus and adjoining the market of Aelia Capitolina. A spacious atrium, the remains of which still stand in the Russian monastery adjoining the present Church of the Holy Sepulchre, gave access to a basilical church. Its apse has been recently uncovered below the pavement of the church. Next came another court, surrounded by columns (their bases were also discovered quite recently). In this court stood the traditional rock of Calvary, surmounted by a huge cross. This second court led to the rotunda (still traceable in the church as it stands today) in the centre of which was the Holy Sepulchre itself. The church was dedicated in 335. Other Constantinian buildings in Jerusalem included the Church of Eleona on the Mount of Olives, of which only the foundations have survived. In Bethlehem the emperor built the Church of the Nativity in the shape of a basilica with five naves, at the end of which an octagonal structure stood over the Grotto of the Nativity. Another church was built at the traditional site of Mamre, north of Hebron.

These imperial structures were soon followed by a flood of others constructed by private donors. In Jerusalem these included the church of St John the Baptist, with a trefoil-shaped plan, the octagon of the Ascension, both of which are still standing, and a basilica at Gethsemane. Other churches were built at Nazareth and Caesarea. Not only were the events related in the New Testament honoured with such memorials, but churches were also built where tradition indicated that the main happenings in the Old Testament—at Shiloh, at Gilgal near Jericho, at the 'Well of Jacob', at Shechem on Mount Gerizim— had occurred. The wave of church building, which ebbed to some extent in the later fifth century, was renewed by the emperor Justinian. He built a splendid Church of the Virgin at Jerusalem (the *Nea* or

▷

Cylindrical two-handled glass flask. 3rd-4th century.
Glass Pavilion. Haaretz Museum.

Two-handled ointment flasks. 4th-5th century.
Glass Pavilion. Haaretz Museum.

◁
Late Roman glass jug. 4th century.

'New Church'). One of the apses of this basilica has recently been excavated in the Jewish quarter of the Old City of Jerusalem. Church building was also energetically pursued in the cities of the Negev wilderness: Nessana has two churches, and so have Avdat and Mampsis while Subeita has three. It has been calculated that in the Byzantine period there was one church for every thousand inhabitants in the cities. Most of the Byzantine churches in Palestine are of the basilical type, with a nave and two aisles separated by colonnades. The entrance is by three doors in the western wall; at the eastern wall there is an apse (sometimes three apses) with an altar; the apse is sometimes contained within the outer wall of the church, and sometimes projects beyond. In some cases, as in the Justinian reconstruction of the Church of the Nativity as it is at present, the three apses were arranged in trefoil shape; but in the Negev they are arranged in parallel. The side apses (or square chambers, if there were no side-apses) served as prothesis and diakonikon, for the ceremony of preparing the Eucharist and the safe keeping of the church treasures. The space before the altar was

separated by a chancel screen from the rest of the church; the screens were often very ornate. Behind the altar was a bench for the clergy, and sometimes a cathedra for the bishop. A preaching pulpit (*ambo*) stood near the chancel screen. This was the standard plan, but there were others: circular, octagonal, cross-shaped churches, and so on.

A tri-apsidal church on the typical plan, with a court (*atrium*), an ante-room (*narthex*), and a connected baptistry, was found at Beth Yerah. It is dated by an inscription to the year 529.

Besides the churches, the building activity of the Byzantines was concentrated on the provision of monasteries, hospices for pilgrims, hospitals and old age homes as works of charity. These were intended for the tens of thousands of pilgrims who now began to flock to the Holy Land. Other measures to the same effect were the safeguarding of the roads by forts and watchtowers. The latter were especially needed on the fringe of the deserts in which many monks chose to dwell as hermits. Whole colonies of such anchorites began to settle in the desert of Judaea. Some lived singly in caves, others created large monasteries, the most famous of which are Mar Saba, Castellion (Mird), and Choziba. Besides the pilgrims who came and returned home, leaving at the most a literary description of their impressions of the Holy Land, others came to settle. The most important group of such newcomers were the refugees from the barbarians who had conquered Italy in the fifth century. They included pious matrons, well-endowed with earthly goods, who proceeded to build monasteries and convents. Others were unfortunates who had to leave the imperial court of Constantinople, the relatives of fallen emperors or ministers in disgrace. The most famous of such exiles was the empress Eudocia, the estranged wife

Jerusalem. Golden Gate. Byzantine gate set up in eastern wall of temple esplanade. Walled up by the Turks as connected with the Messianic aspirations of Christians and Jews.

of the emperor Theodosius II. When she died in Jerusalem in 459 she had spent nearly half a million gold *denarii* on buildings in the city, including a new and larger wall in the south and repairs to the Church of the Holy Sepulchre (or Anastasis, 'Church of the Resurrection', as it was known at that time). She also built a new basilica, that of St Stephen, outside the city walls.

The aspect of Jerusalem and of some of the other cities of Byzantine Palestine has been preserved in the Madaba mosaic map, a sixth-century bird's eye view of the Holy Land. It shows that the city of Jerusalem was bisected by two colonnaded streets starting from a wide square near Damascus Gate, in which stood a column (the gate is still called in Arabic *Bab el Amud,* or 'Gate of the Column'). The main street passed by the Church of the Anastasis and ended at the basilica on Mount Zion, the 'mother of the churches', which was reputed to stand on the site of the Last Supper. Other churches were spread over

the whole city area; one was even built at the south-east corner of the
Temple esplanade, where St James was martyred, according to Christian
tradition. The rest of the esplanade was covered with refuse, as it served
as a city dump.

The transition from a pagan to a Christian empire not only elevated
Palestine to the status of a Holy Land on the spiritual plane; it also had
quite solid material advantages. The influx of pilgrims and sattlers
created a demand for all kinds of goods, in particular perishable food-
stuffs which could not be supplied from afar. In consequence there
arose a strong pressure for an increase in agricultural production and
an extension of cultivated areas. Settlements spread in the Negev,
where five towns: Nessana, Subeita, Elusa, Mampsis (Kurnub) and
Avdat attest, with their Byzantine remains, to the pressing needs of
the period. The inhabitants of these towns cultivated the surrounding lands by a highly sophisticated method of collecting rain water
from a huge area and conducting it by irrigation channels to the fields in
the valleys. They also tended vineyards: the remains of this cultivation,

Heptapegon (et Tabgha). Church of the Multiplication of Loaves and Fishes. Pavement in north wing of transept: bird and city wall. 5th century.

the so-called *tulul el einab* ('little vine hills') can still be observed in regular rows around some of the cities. The Negev cities were not large (Subeita had about 4500 inhabitants, Avdat about 1500) and were not regularly planned. They all, however, had several places of worship and public reservoirs in addition to cisterns in private houses. Clearing the pools was a civic duty imposed on all citizens in turn; we have receipts written on sherds testifying to that effect. In some cases the Byzantines were able to utilize earlier Nabatean houses; owing to the fact that the Negev was not settled after their time, the ruins of the Byzantine houses and churches still sometimes stand up to the second floor or the top of the apse. Nor was life on the Negev bound only by material considerations; papyri found at Nessana attest to the literary pursuits of the inhabitants. Some even studied Virgil in the original, using a Latin-Greek vocabulary. The cities were in contact with the outer world through the pilgrims and trade routes. These routes crisscrossed the Negev and Sinai to Egypt and the Red Sea port of Elath, where Indian goods were delivered by merchantmen. For the

Beth Alpha. Synagogue pavement. The sacrifice of Isaac: Abraham and Isaac. 6th century.

convenience of travellers, public baths were provided near the roads; that at Avdat is one of the better preserved ones.

The art of Byzantine Palestine was mainly ecclesiastical. The basilicas were usually simple in their structure, with architectural ornament in evidence only in their capitals and chancel screens. There were few reliefs, and almost no sculpture in the round. Frescoes or wall mosaics were sometimes applied, but these have mostly perished. The one art which has been preserved in great quantity is that of mosaic pavements, of which a thousand or more have been recorded. The earlier pavements of the churches were severely geometric, probably as a protest against the exuberantly pagan character of the Roman pavements. The representation of the cross and the use of sacred symbols on pavements were forbiddenby a decree of the emperor Theodosius II, issued in 427; evidence of this practice can still be seen in the church of Shavey Zion north of Acre. In the middle of the fifth century a talented mosaic artist laid the pavement at the Church of Heptapegon (et Tabgha) near the Sea of Galilee, a place consecrated as the site of the Miracle of the Loaves and Fishes. The pavements here represent two landscape scenes, based on Nilotic landscapes but adapted to the fauna and flora of the shores of the Sea of Galilee. The figures on this pavement are set down freely against a white background. In later churches the mosaic area is organized in formal geometric patterns, with picture panels. The geometric and floral designs are traditional ones, handed on from generation to generation of mosaic makers from the Hellenistic and Roman periods. The picture panels carefully avoid religious symbols of an overt kind and are mostly medallions filled with animals, surrounded by vine scrolls issuing from an amphora. At Beth Shean, in the monastery founded by a Lady Mary in the sixth century, there are representations of the 'Labours of the Months' arranged in a circle, around a central medallion which shows personifications of the Sun and the Moon. Another pavement in the same group of buildings shows village scenes (the wine-harvest, a wandering Moor with a giraffe, a man playing with his dog). The 'Labours of the Months' are in keeping with the hot climate of the Beth Shean valley: grape-gathering, for instance, is represented both in June and September, instead of the usual autumn picture; sowing is in December. The standard set of mosaic representations is repeated many times in churches all over the country. Near Beth Shean (at el-Hammeh) a pavement repeats the chase and grape-harvest together with the months' pattern, with variations. Occasionally there are also reminders of the old pagan myths, such as Orpheus interpreted allegorically. As the tide of iconoclasm mounted in the sixth century, pavements were mutilated to remove the offending images of man and beast; in one case (at Khirbet Asida near Hebron) the animal patterns were worked over and changed into floral ones. The prevalence of mosaic pavements was not confined to ecclesiastical buildings; many private villas were adorned in the same fashion. One of the finest, of Constantinian date, was found at Beth Guvrin. The central panel represents pairs of animals, a wild and a tame one, dwelling together in peace and amity. Medallions illustrate the four seasons. The border of the pavement is filled with vivid representations of a hunt, from leaving the house to the triumphal return.

Although the Byzantine period was one of Christian rule in high places, the Holy Land became really Christian only in the fifth century, and there were always considerable minorities of Jews and Samaritans living side by side with the Christian population. There was even an attempt made in 363 by the anti-Christian emperor, Julian, to rebuild the Temple; but an earthquake caused the work to be suspended and the death of the emperor, in Persia, put an end to this project. Even after this adversity, the Jews were able to maintain their status in the

P. 138/139

Beth Alpha. Remains of 6th-century synagogue and mosaic pavement. The three panels of the pavement show the Offering of Isaac, a Zodiac and the Ark of the Law.

Beth Shean, Monastery of the Lady Mary. Pavement: of 'Labours of the Months'; head of October. C. AD 569.

Beth Guvrin, Villa. Border of pavement: huntsman. 5th century.

Beth Alpha, synagogue. Border of pavement: bull flanking inscription at entrance. 6th century.

country, and shared in the material prosperity of the Byzantine period. The numerous synagogues of the fourth to seventh centuries attest to this.

The later synagogues differ from the earlier ones in plan, architectural ornament and paving. They were true basilicas, with the apse orientated towards Jerusalem, and the entrance at the opposite side. The Ark of the Covenant, now a solid construction, stood on a platform in the apse, with the community chest below it. A slightly depressed place for prayer stood in front of the Ark, with a chancel screen round it. In contrast to the synagogues of the earlier type, the later ones were bare of any architectural ornament on the outside. The Byzantine laws which forbade the building of new synagogues and only allowed the repair of old ones might have something to do with this external simplicity. Even inside the synagogue architectural ornament was restricted to a few capitals and the chancel screens. As far as we can judge, the interior decoration of the synagogues, apart from possible wall frescoes which have disappeared, consisted of mosaic pavements. The Jewish mosaics were in their early stages as aniconic as those of the early Christian churches and for the same reason—abhorrence of paganism. Gradually, however, a figurative element crept in; because of the lack of any legal restrictions, such as existed in the case of the churches, the makers of synagogue pavements did not hesitate to use biblical scenes. The general Jewish attitude was that the written word was much more sacred than the image; the word represented the actual divine inspiration, whereas the image was only a faint reflection of it. This fact is made abundantly clear if we consider the one certain case of Jewish iconoclasm: in the synagogue of Naaran (Ain Duk) the offending images were carefully removed, while their inscriptions were left untouched.

The pictorial scheme of synagogue pavements of the fifth and sixth centuries reappears frequently with several variations. The central pavement is divided into three sections filled with biblical scenes, followed by a Zodiac with the sun (*Helios*) in the centre and images of the seasons in the corners. The third section, nearest to the apse, shows the Ark of the Covenant, as it were reflected in the floor, flanked by seven-branched candlesticks, lions, palm trees, etc. The biblical scenes refer to some providential act of salvation: the Sacrifice of Isaac (Beth Alpha), Noah's Ark (Gerasa), Daniel in the Lions' Den (Naaran). The choice of the Zodiac was based on more metaphysical considerations: it represented the orderly course of the seasons and of the universe, reflecting both the procession of the feasts as set out in the Law and the divine order of things. In particular the months were connected with the succession of priestly classes serving in the Temple. The image of Helios in his chariot had long since lost all idolatrous significance and had become simply a symbol of the sun. The iconography of the later synagogues shows a definite line of development. The earliest, that of Hammath-Tiberias (early fourth century, by a Constantinian master from Antioch), contains a remarkable series of

P. 142/143
Underground caves near Beth Guvrin in the western Judaean foothills.
The caves were originally quarries for a special type of chalk
much used in Byzantine building activity.

Avdat (Eboda), monastery of the Byzantine period.

*Avdat (Eboda). Ruins
of Church of St Theodore.
Tombstone of Germanos
who died a bachelor aged
17 in* AD *551.*

Avdat (Eboda). Ruins of Church of St Theodore (South Church).
Central apse and chancel screen.

adaptations of Greek images to the standard Zodiac: the Virgin is
Kore with a torch, Libra is Radamantes, the twins are Castor and
Pollux. The ignorance of the Hebrew mosaicist is shown in the sign of
Aquarius, which is depicted the wrong way round, from left to right.

The synagogue of Gaza has an unusual plan of five parallel aisles. In
the central one is the image of King David, dressed as a Byzantine
emperor, but representing Orpheus charming the wild animals. A side
panel shows a series of animals on a scroll. The Gaza synagogue
is dated by an inscription from 508/9. That of Beth Alpha, which
was discovered in 1928, has a bull and a lion guarding the entrance,
and inside can be seen the offering of Isaac, the hand of God visible
from a cloud, Abraham with the knife, Isaac bound and the two
servants standing by with the donkey. The whole is in a very rustic
but most vivid Orientalized style, with the human figures strictly
frontal, ornaments added to the bodies, stylized hair, etc. The Naaran
synagogue (the first pavement to be found, after it had been laid
bare by a shell in 1918) repeats the Beth Alpha pattern in a more
restricted way. Here the representation of Daniel and the lions is
set out in a subsidiary design. Beth Alpha dates from the reign of
Justin (probably the First, 518-27); Naaran might be slightly later.

Subeita (Shivta). Church of St George. The three apses.

The next synagogue chronologically might be Husifa (Isfiye) on Mount Carmel. It has no apse, but its pavement in iconographical sequence stands beyond Beth Alpha in the sixth-century decline in the representation of living beings. The images of the Seasons are still of the usual type such as maidens carrying the symbols of agricultural produce; but the images of the Zodiac are replaced by animals or objects. Aquarius is no longer a man holding a jug, but the jug itself. One interesting item is a representation of peacocks against a background of trellised vines, a motif repeated at Maon. The peacocks have been adopted by Christian, and probably also Jewish, symbolic art as birds of paradise.

The pavement at Maon (Nirim) can be dated to about 530. It shows an interesting adaptation of the standard church pavement with an amphora at the bottom of the design and a vine forming medallions. The latter are filled with symmetrical pairs of animals and various objects, including a bird a cage and vases with fruit, in the central row. Two peacocks flank the amphora. This design, which occurs in the Armenian mosaic at Jerusalem and in the church at Shellal not far from Maon (the Shellal pavement is now at Canberra), has been adopted in Maon, but with a difference. The Christian mosaicists felt that the amphora and vine, and others, were sufficiently symbolic and that the more sacred symbols, for example the Cross and the monogram of Christ and all representations of sacred persons, should be left for the walls of the church where they could not be stepped upon. The synagogue artist refused to acknowledge the symbolic character of the amphora, and hence inserted in the Maon pavement a seven-branched candlestick flanked by lions and palm trees in the side of the pavement nearest to the Ark, together with other Jewish symbols such as the ram's horn (*shofar*) the *lulav* (bunch of leaves), and *ethrog* (citrus) used in the Feast of the Tabernacles.

Only animals are represented in the pavements of the Beth Shean synagogue and that of Hammath-Gader; in fact the latter one had a purely geometric ornament, with the images of two lions as the only details to break its monotony. The two latest synagogues, those of Jericho and Engeddi, represent the last stages of the aniconic process. At Jericho there is a combination of geometric ornament with a few floral elements, a representation of the Ark of the Covenant and the inscription 'Peace upon Israel' with a seven-branched candlestick. At Engeddi, the decorative element has been almost entirely suppressed: the symbols of the Zodiac are replaced by the names of the months. Within two centuries the circle of Jewish figurative mosaics had come back to its point of origin.

Apart from the Jewish synagogues, two Samaritan ones have been discovered, one at Shealvim, orientated towards Mount Gerizim, and a probable one at Beth Shean. As could be expected from their strict adherence to the law of the Pentateuch, the Samaritan synagogues are much more strictly aniconic than the Jewish ones.

A surprising find in a Jewish private house (perhaps used for some public purpose) was made at Beth Shean. The house was paved by a certain Leontis, probably a Jew from Alexandria. The pavement decorations include depictions of the encounter of Odysseus and the Sirens (with the hero duly bound to the mast of his ship), the fight with a sea-monster, and the Nile at Alexandria. The mosaic shows that the Homeric poems were not unknown to the Jews of the fifth century.

In the seventh century Byzantine Palestine underwent a series of crises. The dogmatic struggles of the fifth century between the Orthodox and

Nirim, Synagogue of Ma'on, near Gaza. Pavement: leopard, 6th century.

the Monophysites had created a rift in the Christian majority, which remained unhealed. The strong rule of Justinian drove the Samaritans to revolt, with the resulting destruction of many churches. In 614 the Persians invaded Palestine and were helped by a Jewish revolt. The invaders occupied Jerusalem, where all churches (including that of the Holy Sepulchre) were destroyed. After the Persian retreat in 627, the emperor Heraclius and the local patriarch Modestus restored some of the churches. In 630 the Muslim invasion from Arabia began. Jerusalem fell in 638 and within two years the whole of the Holy Land was under Muslim rule.

The Arabs (640-1099)

The new rulers of Palestine were accepted by the majority of the population with good will, as they had shown themselves both strong and tolerant. They granted to all those submitting to the rule of Islam the preservation of their lives, the enjoyment of their possessions, freedom of religious worship, and freedom from billeting, the whole against payment of a poll tax. As they had no administrative apparatus at their disposal, the Muslims continued to use the existing Byzantine system. On the papyri of Nessana one can still distinguish the spidery strokes of the Greek clerks from the broad and bold Arabic writing of the victors.

Bedouin tents.

While the damage done during the conquest was quickly repaired in most of the area, the economy of the Negev was ruined beyond repair. Themselves the sons of Bedouins, the Caliphs naturally favoured the desert nomads roaming at the edge of the settled area over the town-dwellers. Gradually the security which made settlement in the south possible was accordingly undermined, and the exodus of the settlers began. Moreover, with the reduction of the stream of pilgrims and of capital accretions, there was less need for cultivated land. The caravan roads were deserted and the cities gradually emptied of their inhabitants. There was no compulsion behind this; the Nessana papyri show the interest taken by the Arab governors in these regions. A striking example of tolerance can still be seen at Subeita, where a mosque was added outside the southern church without disturbing the Christian edifice in any significant way.

The same spirit of tolerance was shown by the Caliph Umar when he took Jerusalem. Leaving the Church of the Holy Sepulchre untouched, he proceeded to the Temple esplanade and himself began to carry away the accumulated rubbish, with the assistance of the patriarch Sophronius. In the end the Rock in the centre of the esplanade (once probably the foundation of the altar of burnt offerings) was laid bare. The Muslims, however, chose to set up a place for prayer at the southern end of the esplanade, on the side facing Mecca. There they set 'great beams on some ruins and made a quadrangular place of prayer which could hold three thousand men at once'. This was the earliest el-Aqsa mosque, the one 'most removed' (from Mecca), from which one night the prophet Mohammed started his voyage to heaven, according to Muslim tradition.

The status of Palestine was much improved following establishment of the Umayyad dynasty by Muawiyya in 661. The new caliph had himself crowned at Jerusalem; and from their capital at Damascus the Umayyad caliphs did much to develop their southern possessions. In the time of the caliph Abd-el-Malik (685-705), Mecca was in the hands of his opponent Abdallah Ibn Zubayr; in order to diminish the flow of pilgrims in that direction, the caliph decided to create a new centre of pilgrimage in Jerusalem and built the Dome of the Rock (Qubbat es-Sakhra, wrongly called the 'Mosque of Omar'). The building was completed in 691 and is the earliest monument of Muslim architecture still standing.

To understand the plan of the Dome of the Rock we must go back to the intentions of its builder. Besides the will to create a substitute for the sanctuary at Mecca, Abd-el-Malik also intended to outdo Constantine by creating a second dome in Jerusalem besides that standing over the Holy Sepulchre. The most sacred visible part of the Temple esplanade was the rock in its centre; hence a dome (20.4 m. in diameter and 35.3 m. high) was erected over it on a drum, supported by four piers and twelve columns; the drum was pierced with sixteen windows. This circular structure was enclosed within an octagon, each face 20.6 m. in length, with doors on four of its eight sides and windows in the other four.

As the distance between the octagon and the inner circle of columns supporting the dome was structurally too great, an inner octagon was inserted with twenty-four arches resting on eight piers and sixteen columns. The dome, the arches and the walls over the inner circle were decorated with a rich pattern of mosaics, derived from Byzantine prototypes but omitting all except floral and geometric ornament. The remainder of the walls was covered with marble; the tie beams of the arches, and the beams over the doors, were decorated with gilt floral motifs. The outer faces of the octagon were covered with faience by the Turkish sultan Suleiman in 1552; the roof is of lead and the dome has been recently gilded. The caliph assigned seven years of the revenue of Egypt for this building, and summoned workmen from Egypt and apparently also from Syria. The whole structure is a remarkable

▷

Dome of the Rock seen through the arches of porch enclosing Temple Mount.

Dome of the Rock.

P. 158/159
Dome over the Rock, seen from below, with its rich gilt stylized ornament.

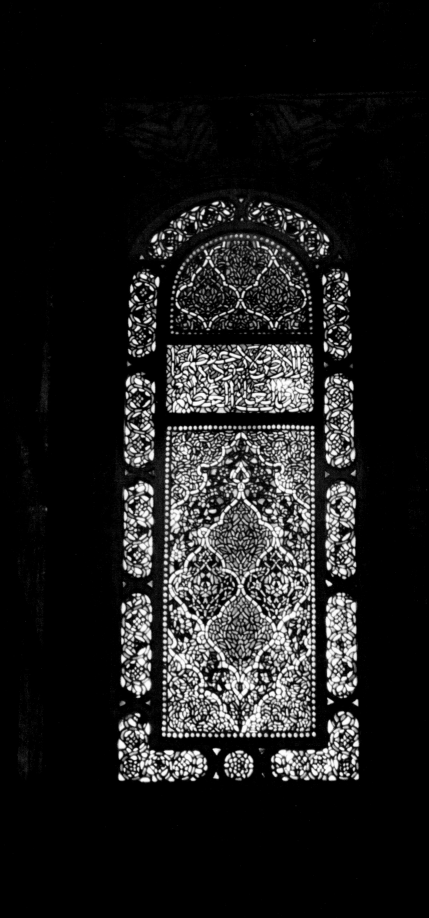

achievement of architectural harmony and elegance, combining grandeur in the plan with minute delicacy in the details.

The inscription commemorating Abd-el-Malik was later changed, his name being replaced by that of the Abbasid caliph al-Ma'mun; but as the forger forgot to change the date (72 of the Hijra, i.e. 691) this fraud proved ineffective.

Among the other works of the Umayyads in Palestine is the foundation of the city of Ramla in 712 as the administrative capital of the province by the governor, Suleiman. This is the only city in Palestine founded by the Arabs. Its name is derived from the word meaning sand, as it was built on sandy soil. The city developed industries such as pottery and dyeing and was soon flourishing.

The other buildings of the Umayyads were secular in character, apart from the enlargement and remaking of the original el-Aqsa mosque. The Umayyads still maintained links with their Bedouin past, and lived for some months each year in the desert—even if they preferred desert palaces to the tents of the true Bedouins. The caliphs Walid I (705-13) and Hisham (724-43) also constructed winter palaces in the warm climate of the Jordan Valley, which they preferred to their capital, Damascus, which was uncomfortably cold in winter. One such palace was built by Walid at Sinnabra, near Beth Yerah where the Jordan River issues from the Sea of Galilee, of which nothing now remains visible. The second palace by Walid was built near Magdala on the shores of the same sea, at a place called Horvat Minnim (Khirbet el-Minya in Arabic). The palace was shaped like a rectangular fortress, (73 by 63 m.) with round towers in the corners and semi-circular ones in the centre of each side. There was an ornate and elaborate gateway between two towers on the east. There is a mosque on the southern side (also accessible from the outside), a throne room and a group of five ceremonial halls paved with geometric mosaics. The dwelling rooms are on the north, with functional spaces (guard-rooms, etc.) in the east and west. The upper storey is reached by a ramp near the gate.

Another Umayyad palace has been excavated in the Jordan Valley at Khirbet Mefjer, north of Jericho. This is a huge complex which has an entrance gate leading to a forecourt within which stands an ornamental pool. The forecourt leads to the main court of the palace through a gate richly ornamented with stucco designs. The palace consists of dwelling rooms (including an underground bath paved with mosaics for an agreeable sojourn in the burning heat of the summer). There is a small mosque for the use of the caliph in the southern wall; attached to it is a square minaret tower (all the other towers of the palace compound are either round or semi-circular). The palace also includes, on its northern side, a large reception hall divided into two by a row of pillars. Adjoining the palace on the north is a large public mosque and an elaborate building which seems to have been the throne hall. It has an ornamental gate, domed over, and two series of vaults surrounding a central dome. Besides this hall is a smaller bath, one room of which is paved with a very fine mosaic showing a lion attacking gazelles under a 'tree of life'. The throne hall is paved with a bewildering variety of mosaic pavements with geometric designs. Most of the decoration of the palace is carved in stucco, with motifs (mainly of Persian origin) of enormous richness. Of the greatest interest are the figures in the round found

◁
Stained glass window in the Dome of the Rock.

Dome of the Rock. Pillar of inner octagon, with marble plating arranged into ornaments and mosaics of the drum behind, showing an arabesque evolution of the Byzantine stylized vine trellis issuing from an amphora.

in profusion in the palace, especially in the throne room. It had already been found through excavations at Qusayr Amra and other sites that the Umayyads allowed paintings with figurative representations in their palaces. The use of three-dimensional sculpture was, however, a new facet of their antinomism. The sculptures include a representation of the caliph himself, a bearded figure resplendent in his Persian robes; this figure apparently stood over the gateway of the throne hall. Other carvings show soldiers with Oriental and Roman armour, semi-nude dancers, heads used for the decoration of the cupola, birds, etc. They are painted in many colours and the whole decor must have been full of life but somewhat garish in character. The geometric and floral ornament of the windows and balustrades, on the other hand, is in the finest taste. This palace was built with the help of Christian and Jewish labourers, as is shown by graffiti found on the site.

The Umayyad dynasty was replaced in 750 by the Abbasids, who chose Baghdad as their residence. Owing to this transfer of the capital from Damascus, Palestine became somewhat neglected in this period. The

Dome of the Rock. Part of ornament on underside of intercolumnar beams. Classical elements are arranged in a stylized pattern.

Khirbet Mefjer. Palace of the Caliph Hisham (724-43). Columns and pillars of the throne room.

Abbasid caliphs, al-Mahdi and ez-Zahir, transformed the el-Aqsa mosque. Under al-Mahdi the mosque became a large rectangular building with a central nave leading to the dome and the *mihrab* (niche pointing to Mecca), with seven aisles and as many entrances on each side. Part of his plan was followed by later architects; the roof-beams and wall-plates of this period have been preserved. The mosque was dedicated in 780, when the caliph came to Jerusalem to pray.

A more abiding monument from the Abbasid era is the cistern of el Uneiziyye at Ramla completed in 789. It is built on an irregular four-sided plan (24 x 20.5 m.), with three rows of piers inside. The piers form six vaulted halls, each subdivided into four cells, twenty-four in all. Each cell had its opening in the roof, so that twenty-four persons could draw water simultaneously. The architectural innovation here is the use of the pointed arch, the earliest surviving example of the systematic employment of this device, which spread all over Europe in the Middle Ages.

The later Abbasid period marks the beginning of the decline of Arab rule. Power was seized by commanders of their Seljuk or Turkish mercenaries, while the caliph became more and more of a puppet. The neglected western provinces broke away from the Muslim empire. Thus Ahmad ibn Tulun, the son of a Turkish slave, became the ruler of Egypt and Palestine; he and his successors erected many buildings, few of which have survived. The Tulunids were followed by the Fatimids, descendants of Muhammad's daughter Fatima, who denied

Khirbet Mefjer. Stucco balustrades in the Umayyad palace.

Khirbet Mefjer. Centrepiece of dome in stucco. Stylized flower in centre, surrounded by heads of men and women. Rockefeller Museum.

Khirbet Mefjer. Reconstructed stucco window from façade of Hisham's palace. Rockefeller Museum.

Ramla (789). Abbasid cistern, called el Uneiziyye, a very early example of pointed arches.

Dome of el-Aqsa seen above south wall of Temple esplanade, with its mixed Herodian, Umayyad and Turkish masonry. The Herodian part is left below, the Turkish is on top. The rest is Umayyad.

the legitimacy of the Abbasid caliphate (969-1171). It was the Fatimid ez-Zahir who gave the el-Aqsa mosque its present form in 1035. Of his work the following survive: the central aisle, the arches under the dome with their mosaics and the central doorway. The seven-aisled mosque is based on Zahir's plan, even if it was largely rebuilt in the time of the Crusaders and again in the present century, during the 1930s. The façade is Ayyubid and dates from 1217/18. The mosaics in the dome imitate those of the Dome of the Rock, but belong to the time of ez-Zahir.

Zahir's predecessor Hakim (996-1020) gained a less enviable renown by ordering the destruction of the Church of the Holy Sepulchre, which was rebuilt in the eleventh century by the emperor of Byzantium. The decline of Fatimid rule was marked by the rise of the Seljuk Turks, who proceeded to oppress and plunder the Christian pilgrims to the Holy Sites. When news of this reached Europe, the Pope and the monks called upon the knights of Europe to save the Holy Sepulchre from the infidels; thus began the movement known as the Crusades, which has left its mark on the face of the Holy Land until this day.

The Crusaders (1099-1291)

The First Crusade, the only one fully to accomplish its aims, started in 1096 as a joint French-Norman expedition, assisted by the Italian seafaring cities. After much suffering the survivors stormed Jerusalem on 15 July 1099 and established the Latin Kingdom of Jerusalem, the principal Crusader state. The kingdom was consolidated by Baldwin I (1100-18) who extended its boundaries by securing the coastal cities. At its greatest extent, in the reign of Baldwin III, the Crusader dominion comprised the whole of the coast down to Ascalon. Inland it included the heights east of the Jordan down to the Red Sea. A chain of fortresses from Shaubak to the Isle de Grave protected it on this side.

The Crusader kingdom was dominated by a few thousand Europeans ruling over many more Orientals, some Christian, some Muslim. Most of the knights who had fought in the first and subsequent crusades went home once they had fulfilled their vows, leaving the kingdom to its fate. The kings reigning at Jerusalem had to conform to the European social model, the only type of society they knew. They organized the kingdom on a feudal basis, distributing the lands to their vassals: the Prince of Galilee, the Seigneurs of Haifa, Jaffa, Caesarea, Ybellin (Yavneh), etc. As these noblemen were only bound to furnish service for a stated period of days in the year, the kings were chronically short of military power. The Italian colonies, which dominated the coastal towns, consisted mainly of merchants and could at best simply supply the vital maritime link with Europe. The Oriental Christians in the Crusader kingdom were dissatisfied because they were under the spiritual rule of the Latin Church, while they themselves followed the Orthodox rite. The Muslims could at best be expected to remain passive. In these difficult circumstances the establishment of the Military Orders (Templars, Hospitallers, the Teutonic Order) furnished, from the first half of the twelfth century, a standing army which became the backbone of the Crusader state. From the time of Fulk of Anjou (1134-43), the Crusaders were on the defensive; the Muslims, whose divisions were one of the main causes of the success

Armorial lion of Crusader king of the Lusignan family, found at Acre. Rockfeller Museum.

of the First Crusades, were gradually united under the Ayyubids, and took the offensive, which was sustained by the great Kurdish warrior Saladin for twenty-two years. He achieved his greatest success at the Horns of Hattin (1187) when the Crusader army, divided by internal disputes, was overwhelmed, the king captured, and Jerusalem taken. Everything seemed lost until the situation was partly saved by the Third Crusade. Acre was recaptured by the Crusaders in 1191 and became the capital of the kingdom in its second phase. The Crusaders profited from disunion among the Ayyubids and gradually regained Galilee, the coast and, for a time (1229-44), even Jerusalem, but more by diplomacy than by force of arms. The later Crusades were defensive in character. After the rise of the Mamelukes and their triumphs over the Ayyubids in 1250, the end was near. The energetic sultan Baybars (1260-79) captured one Crusader fortress after another. His second successor, al-Malik al-Ashraf, took Acre in 1291 and thereby ended the era of the Crusades.

In order to understand the culture of the Crusades and the character of their surviving monuments, we have to keep in mind the following: the Crusaders were mainly French, with an admixture of Normans and Germans. They brought with them the cultural and

Crusader architectural details re-used in Mameluke.
pulpit on the Temple Mount.

artistic standards of Medieval Europe in the eleventh century. As time went on and they settled in their new domains, they began a cultural exchange with the Orientals among whom they lived. This was especially notable as regards the comforts of life, in which the Orient was at that time vastly superior to anything Europe could show. Then, by the very nature of their slender tenure on the land they conquered, the Crusaders had above all to consider their security, hence the enormous amount of energy and means used to build one fortress after another. In the field the Latin kingdom could not, unless supported by the occasional assistance of European Knights, stand up to the masses of Muslim warriors. They had to seek safety in strongholds which could not be captured by a sudden cavalry raid.

Moreover the Crusades had a spiritual motivation. Whatever mundane motives might have got mixed up in them—lust for adventure, or hope of lands and riches—the dominant incentive was idealistic: the delivery of the Holy Sites from the Muslim yoke. Hence, once established in the Holy Land, the Crusaders devoted hardly less energy to church building than to the erection of fortifications. To this day the principal mosques of many Arab cities, such as Gaza, Ramla, Lydda, are Crusader churches transformed into sanctuaries of another faith. Even

▷
12th-century Crusader church of St Anne,
interior in Romanesque style. Jerusalem.

the fabric of the el-Aqsa mosque dates mostly from the Crusader period. The tremendous energy shown by the European settlers is evident here also.

In their art, the Crusaders followed European masters, mostly of Burgundy and Provence, as well as Oriental and Byzantine executants. Their earlier churches were Romanesque in style; and some of their finest sculpture, such as the capitals found at Nazareth, are master-pieces of Late Romanesque art. Towards the end of their rule, the Gothic style appears in some Crusader churches; it is a disputed point among scholars whether they took over the pointed arch from such Muslim prototypes as the Ramla cistern. In other arts the Crusaders had to rely on the Byzantines. Thus the mosaics applied to the walls of the Church of the Nativity at Bethlehem and that of the Holy Sepulchre are the work of Byzantine mosaicists, similar to those who worked for the Norman kings in Sicily; some of the inscriptions are bilingual, Greek and Latin. Of these mosaics those at Bethlehem are now hardly visible; in the Calvary chapel of the Holy Sepulchre, a panel showing Christ Pantocrator survives among many modern mosaics. The Crusaders' glazed pottery was the work of Byzantine potters, with some imitation of the Mameluke prototypes. The glaze is greenish or yellow, with floral and geometric design combined with images of men, beasts and ships.

The Crusaders' building activity was of course most prominent in Jeru-salem. They rebuilt the Church of the Holy Sepulchre, adding its present façade. The lintels of the two doors of the church represent Christ's entry into Jerusalem, the Last Supper, the Raising of Lazarus, etc. on one lintel, while the other shows a complicated scroll with interspersed human figures, recalling antique 'peopled scrolls'. Within the church the ambulatory was added to the rotunda and the Calvary chapel built over the rock of Golgotha. Other Crusader churches in the capital are the Church of St Anne, and the traditional Tomb of the Virgin Mary in the Kidron Valley. St Anne, which was probably built by the masons of the Holy Sepulchre, is still the best preserved Crusader church in Jerusalem; there are similarities in design in the west façade and the window above it. The church is built in pure Romanesque style, with the nave ending under a small dome. The Church of the Tomb of the Virgin still has its twelfth-century entrance, and inside a vaulted cruciform crypt contains an empty sarcophagus. Crusader reliefs (with the Cross carefully removed) are to be found re-used in the Dome of the Rock (the cave below the rock) and in the el-Aqsa mosque. A few architectural details of some of the churches near the Hospital (a *voussoir* with the signs of the Zodiac and frag-ments of a tympanum) are built into the wall of the modern church near the Holy Sepulchre. Another Crusader church which has been partly restored stands at Abu Ghosh, 12 km. west of Jerusalem. It has the normal inner division into nave, aisles and a triple apse. Because of its isolated position the walls were exceptionally thick (4 m.) so that it could be used as a fortress in case of need. A spring below the church has been included in a crypt 14.2 by 7.5 m. One special feature of Crusader churches is the belfry; the Oriental churches did not use bells, but the Latin churches did so. One such belfry stood near the

▷

Crusader tower and walls of the Citadel, Jerusalem; formerly called David's Tower.

entrance to the Church of the Holy Sepulchre; its upper storey was dismantled under Muslim rule so as not to stand higher than the mosque nearby. At Bethlehem, where the Crusader cloisters have been partly preserved through being enclosed within more recent pillars, a set of bells from the Middle Ages has also been unearthed.

The civil and military architecture of the Crusades left numerous remains scattered all over the country. These have suffered much from later building activities, as their walls were used as quarries, but they have not been put to other uses, as happened to the Crusader churches all over the country. In Jerusalem the present day shape of the Citadel and part of its outer walls and towers date back to the Crusader period. The king of Jerusalem originally resided in the el-Aqsa mosque, to which various additions were made to transform it into a palace. When the Templars took over the Temple Mount, the king established himself near 'David's Tower'—the one Herodian tower

Caesarea. Crusader wall, built in 1251 by St Louis of France. The curtain wall (now ruined) stood on the sloping bastioned base with fosse in front.

which was still standing near Jaffa Gate. In this he unwittingly followed
in the footsteps of the Jewish king as well as of the Roman governors
who succeeded him. The Crusader remains at the other capital, Acre,
are more numerous. There is a fragment of the Crusader sea-wall still
in use. Recent excavations have uncovered the refectory of the Order
of St John, a vast hall with cross-vaultings resting on a row of three
pillars, each of which is 3 m. in diameter. The hall was connected by
underground passages with several other rooms, as yet unexplored.

The Crusader walls of Caesarea, built under the direction of Louis IX
(Saint Louis) of France, are still the best preserved city walls of
that period. They are composed of an outer wall 4-6 m. high, a fosse
7 m. broad, a glacis 8 m. high and inclined at 60°, and an inner wall
10 m. high. The whole is modelled on the Byzantine walls of Constantinople, then the strongest fortress in the Christian world. The walls
form a rectangle, 650 by 275 m. There were two gates in the north

P. 180/181
Crusader vaulted street at Caesarea leading from gate inside city.

Belvoir fortress (1168), seen from a distance.

and south (the former with a small bridge over the fosse supported by a single pillar) and a main gate in the centre of the eastern wall. The gate is reached by a bridge over the fosse. The inner half of the bridge is built on an arch, while the outer half was of wooden planks, easily removable. Once over the bridge the attackers had to present their unprotected right flank to the gate tower and to make a right-angled turn to enter the gate. The gate itself is vaulted over and issues on an arched-over street. Not far from the gate were the remains of a Crusader cathedral, which was planned on a huge scale but left unfinished.

Three Crusader castles have been well preserved and illustrate the methods of fortification of the three principal orders. The oldest is that of Belvoir (*Kokhav ha-Yarden,* in Arabic, *Kaukab el-Hawa*) which was built by the Hospitallers from 1168 onwards on a high mountain overlooking the Jordan Valley south of the Sea of Galilee. The fortress was separated on three sides from the spur on which it stands by a fosse, 20 m. wide and 12 m. deep. The eastern side, which drops down sharply to the Jordan valley, is secured by a high glacis. The main entrance is from the south-east by a bridge over the fosse and a complicated system of gateways. The fortress itself consists of an outer pentagon and an inner square. The outer fortifications include a curtain wall with high battlements and square towers at the corners and centre of each face. The eastern tower, which stands at the apex of the pentagon, was an immensely powerful stronghold by itself. The vaults along the curtain walls are spacious and provide for a strong garrison. A bath house and a large cistern (500 cubic metres) are situated in the outer court. The square inner fortress has square towers in the corners and a gate tower in the centre of the west side. Within were a bakery and kitchen, vaulted rooms, and a church on the second storey, with a tower nearby. Some of the sculptures of the church have been recovered, including an angel symbolizing St John the Evangelist in high relief, with a grotesque, grinning face.

In two later fortresses, those of Montfort and the Safed citadel, the square towers of Belvoir were replaced by round ones. Apparently the knights had learned by experience that a round tower gave a better field of fire by eliminating dead ends, and was also more likely to withstand the deadly mangonels of the Mamelukes. Athlith castle (Château des Pèlerins) was built by the Templars with the assistance of pilgrims of the Fifth Crusade in 1218. It has an outer wall with square towers beyond a fosse which could be flooded from the sea. The inner wall has two very high towers which dominate the outer defences. Inside there are vaulted halls and an octagonal church resembling the Dome of the Rock—the 'Temple of Solomon' in Crusader eyes. The castle was inexpugnable so long as the Crusaders commanded the sea and in fact never fell but was evacuated by the knights after the fall of Acre in 1291.

The castle of Montfort was built by the Teutonic order in 1228 on a mountain spur overlooking two valleys in Galilee. A deep fosse was cut in the spur, separating the castle from its surroundings. From the strategic point of view the castle was worthless, but it was not planned, like Belvoir, to dominate an extensive area, but was chosen by the Teutonic Order as the place to keep treasure and archives in safety.

◁
Belvoir. View of Jordan Valley.

Belvoir. Door and arrow-slits. with view of the Jordan Valley dominated by the fortress.

The castle was built so that its strongest tower, the keep, a huge oval construction, stood over the fosse at the point most vulnerable for the defenders. The remainder of the castle spreads on terraces descending towards the Keziv Valley. Below the workshops and the dwelling rooms of the knights comes the church, 23 by 8 m., with octagonal piers supporting its pointed vaults. This is followed by the chapter hall, a square room also built on piers, with vaulted cellars underneath. The castle is defended at its western end by a round bastion. The whole is enclosed by a thick outer wall with round towers.

Acre. Refectory of the Order of St John (Hospitallers).
The vaults rest on three huge pillars.

The castle was used till 1271, when it fell to the Mamelukes; the archives of the order were transferred first to Acre and then to Europe, where the Teutonic order continued to play an important historical role. In fact the former kingdom of Prussia may be said to have had its origin in the walls of 'Starkenburg', as Montfort was called in German.

In the whole history of the Holy Land the Crusades remain an episode: a crumbling wall, some vaults open to the sky, rusty armour and pieces of coloured glass found in excavations are all the material remains to be found in an area for which so much blood was shed. The permanent effects of the episode can be traced in European history, in the beginning of the decay of feudalism, the rise of the cities, the increased trade in Oriental goods, the rise in the standard of everyday comfort, the new materials and types of goods now produced. These were the main results of the efforts

Montfort. Ruins of the fortress of the Teutonic Order in Upper Galilee (1228).

of the doughty knights who repose under their brasses in the European churches, their knees crossed to show that they had performed their duty as Christian warriors. They had not learned the simple truth that it is not enough to occupy a country by military strength, and that to make an occupation permanent one has to labour for it with the sweat of one's brow.

The Mamelukes (1291-1516)

Like matter and anti-matter in modern physics, the Crusading knights had a counter-force, the Mameluke rulers of Egypt. The Ayyubids, of whom Saladin was the most renowned, were in the end unable to evict the Frankish knights even after they had restored Jerusalem to Islam. The last Ayyubid in Egypt was deposed in 1250 and the reins were taken over by the commander of his Turkish bodyguard, an ex-slave or Mameluke (literally 'one who was once owned'). Thus arose a type of government for which there is no parallel in history. The Mamelukes were all formerly slaves of sultans or amirs. At first they were mainly of Turkish origin; after 1390, when the supply of Turkish slaves ran out, they were mostly Circassians from the Caucasus. Each was called by the name of his former owner, and most were converts to Islam. Only former Mamelukes could become sultans: their descendants were thought fit only for civil functions and merged with the rest of the people. As could be expected of a military caste, Mameluke rule was exceedingly turbulent. Sultans were made and deposed with astonishing speed, and their amirs often shared the same fate. The historians distinguish two Mameluke dynasties: the Bahris ('of the Nile', because their barracks were near the river), who were Turks, and the Burjis ('of the citadel', of Cairo, where they had their headquarters) or Circassians. In the latter dynasty

Porticoes (riwaqs) *bordering the Temple Mount.*

it has been calculated that fourteen sultans reigned in the space of nine years.

Till they met their fate under Ottoman artillery at Merj Dabiq in 1516, the Mamelukes were most efficient warriors. One of the earliest of their rulers, Baybars (1260-77) was the bane of the Crusader kingdom, although Acre only fell to his second successor. It was Baybars who established a systematic policy of 'scorched earth' in the coastal areas. In order to prevent the possibility of a Crusader landing—for the sea was still ruled by the Christian fleets—he had all the cities on the coast and all the castles razed, and the whole area was handed over to Turkoman shepherds as grazing ground. In the interior, the Mameluke viceroys were established at Gaza and Safed, while Jerusalem was relegated to second rank, being regarded mainly as a place of honourable banishment for amirs who had fallen out of grace at the court in Cairo, but did not, as yet, deserve to be executed. They settled in the Holy City and by their donations and buildings helped enhance its Islamic character, in particular in the areas of the Old City adjoining the Haram esh-Sherif (Temple Mount).

For all their turbulence and restlessness, the Mamelukes were in the beginning most efficient rulers. They established a system of caravanserais and postal relays between Cairo and Damascus. Remains of their square khans (caravanserais) with towers in their corners can still be observed at Rosh ha-Ayin near the sources of the Yarkon river, at Khan Yunis near Gaza and at Khan et-Tujjar near Mount Tabor.

Jerusalem. The Lions' Gate, flanked by the armorial lions of Baybars.

The roads connecting these khans were well kept and provided with bridges. One of these, Jisr Jindas just north of Lydda, still bears the heavy airport traffic; it is adorned by an inscription of Baybars flanked by his mark, a pair of lions. The same mark can be observed on both sides of the Lions' Gate, the eastern gate of the Old City of Jerusalem. Another of the Mameluke gates of Jerusalem is the Damascus Gate.

Public fountain (sabil) *of the Sultan Qayt-Bay (1482) on the Temple Mount. The alternating layers of red and white stones, ornate inscriptions and decorated dome are typical of Mameluke architecture at its finest.*

Flanked by ornamental towers and following the ground-plan of the Roman gate underneath, this gate, with its plethora of needlelike battlements, is one of the finest monuments of the period.

Paradoxically enough, for all their martial bearing and turbulent spirits, the Mamelukes had impeccable taste and employed the very best artists, architects and artisans. When they proceeded to surround the

Entrances and gateways of Mameluke buildings in the Old City, in street leading to the Gate of the Chain and the Temple Mount.

P. 196/197
Entrance portal to the Madrasa al-Ashrafiyye adjoining the Temple Mount. Notable is the bichrome masonry and stalactite ornament of dome.

Haram esh-Sherif (the Temple Mount) with a solid ring of Muslim *madrasas* (schools of theology), *zawiyas* (Derwish monasteries), *ribats* (hospices), palaces and mausoleums, they placed the seal of their peculiar type of architecture over much of what was still left of medieval Jerusalem. The façades of the Mameluke buildings were constructed of alternating rows of red and white stone in which were inserted friezes of elaborate dedicatory inscriptions with Koranic passages in the flowing naskhi script of medieval Arabic. Here and there were inserted the arms of the various amirs, indicating the functions they had filled at court: a cup for the cup-bearer, polo sticks for the polo master, a napkin for the chamberlain (*jamdar*), a set of writing materials for the *dawadar* or secretary. Round shields with ornate arabesques were placed in relief on the walls to relieve their flatness. The entrances of the Mameluke foundations are high semi-domes adorned with stalactite patterns. Among the resplendent Mameluke buildings in Jerusalem we find the Madrasa Ashrafiyya (called after al-Malik al-Ashraf), Qayt-Bay (1482), and opposite it near the Dome of the Rock his public fountain (*sabil*), which is the finest Mameluke monument in Jerusalem. In the Street of the Chain leading to the Haram the amir Tankiz built the Madrasa Tankiziyya (1328/9), one of the best preserved of the Mameluke monuments in Jerusalem. Slightly west in the same street is the mausoleum of the Lady Tunshuk (Sitt Tunshuk) who died in 1398; its façade is ornamented with an intricate arabesque design.

Outside Jerusalem, at Ramla, is the White Mosque, a complex of buildings set within a large enclosure (93 by 84 m.). The mosque proper stands to the south. It is a long building with thirteen doors, partly Umayyad and partly Ayyubid, which was flanked by long porticoes, now mainly in ruins, running along the east and west sides. The main gate was on the east. In the centre of the courtyard are two vast cisterns with pointed arches forming cross-vaults. The Tower ('Minaret') of Ramla, still a conspicuous landmark, was built by the Mameluke sultan Qalaun (1318) on the north side of the complex. Other Mameluke buildings in Safed include the Red Mosque (al-Jami' al-Ahmar) built by Baybars in 1275, and the Zawiyat Bani Hamid, a tomb of the amir Muzaffar-ad-din Musa (1372).

Jerusalem. Mameluke lion in court of Rockefeller Museum.

Medieval streets in the old city of Jerusalem.

The Ottomans, 1516 to the Nineteenth Century

In 1516 the Mameluke army was destroyed by the janissaries and the artillery of Sultan Selim I the Grim (Yawuz) of the Ottoman dynasty. The Holy Land fell into the hands of the Turks in the same year and remained a Turkish province for exactly four hundred years. Culturally, however, the Ottoman period can be divided into two stages: the period of Oriental culture up to the nineteenth century, and the period of ever-growing European influence thereafter, until the end of Ottoman rule.

The new government, in the sixteenth century, was at first a haven of stability under the first two sultans, Selim I and his son Suleiman I the *Qanuni* ('Lawgiver'), known in Europe as Suleiman the Magnificent (1520-66). Suleiman in particular carried out a thorough reorganiz-ation of the province. He repaired the walls of the Old City of Jerusalem and gave them the shape they still keep. An inscription on Jaffa Gate, and several more dispersed along the walls, attest to this fact. Within the city and on the dam which leads up to 'Mount Zion', Suleiman had *sabils* (public fountains) constructed, ornamented with reliefs in arabesque and stalactite semi-domes, with pointed arches and chevrons over them. Later monuments of the Ottoman Period in Jerusalem include the Golden Gate, the eastern gate of the Temple Mount. This was kept open in Crusader and Mameluke times; but because of the popular belief that the Messiah would arrive by way of this gate, the Turks had it walled up, decorating the tower above the Byzantine arched lintel with their circular ornaments. Suleiman also had the outer face of the octagon of the Dome of the Rock covered with faience tiles, bringing Armenian workers from Kutahiye (Asia Minor) for this purpose. The elegant grey-blue faience of the exterior of the Dome formed a striking contrast with the gilt cupola above it.

The early promises of Ottoman rule, however, were soon belied. After the death of Suleiman, a succession of weak sultans and corrupt viziers let the country disintegrate. The pashas not only exacted from the hapless subjects a heavy and swelling price for any public appoint-ment, but were constantly waging war on each other and on the local chieftains. Occasionally the sultans at Constantinople lost practically all control. This was the situation in the days of the Druze emir Fakhr ad-Din in the sixteenth century, and again in the eighteenth in the time

▷

Turkish buildings in the Jerusalem citadel (16th century).

P. 202/203
Eastern wall of Jerusalem, with blocked Golden Gate and Muslim cemetery in front.

of the Bedouin Dahir el-Umar, who ruled over Galilee from his resi-
dence in Acre, which he fortified. He built the walls of Tiberias and
the fortress north of its old city. Dahir allied himself with the
Egyptian ruler Ali Bey, and with the Russians, then at war with the
Turks. At the time of his death in 1775, he ruled over almost the whole
of Palestine. He was succeeded in the same year by the Bosnian
Ahmed Pasha, called el-Jazzar ('the Butcher') because of his cruelty.
Jazzar ruled over northern Palestine from Acre until his death in 1804.
He is known in world history as the man who thwarted Napoleon's
attempts to capture Acre, and thereby diverted the Corsican from his
course of conquering the Orient to ruling Europe. Jazzar made great
efforts to embellish Acre in accordance with the Turkish taste of his
period; it was largely due to him that the 'rococo' style of Ottoman
culture is represented in Palestine. His mosque at Acre is modelled
on the praying houses of imperial Istanbul; it is the only mosque in
Palestine to have a minaret of the tall and slender type, which
varies the sky-line of Istanbul in such a pleasant manner. Within, the
mosque was laid out in the Ottoman manner with designs in black and
white marble. For his colonnades Jazzar shamelessly plundered the
ruins of Caesarea. His fountain outside the mosque is an elegant
example of rococo Turkish. His tomb is surmounted by the turban
of the true believer, with its sides ornamented by baskets and vases
of fruit, represented in relief. The mosque stands in a court surrounded by a small dome. The 'Bath of the Pasha' nearby is a classic example
of a Turkish bath of the traditional type. It is now a museum.
After the siege by Napoleon, who had made an assault on the walls
of Acre built by Dahir el-Umar, Jazzar fortified the city with a complicated pattern of walls, fosses and counterscarps, designed to ward
off any future attacker. His successor Suleiman (1804-18) further developed Acre, providing it with a new bazaar. Jazzar also built a khan
in Acre (one of the two which are still standing). It was to serve the
growing commercial needs of the city and ensure its development as
a centre of trade in the Levant. One of the Turkish sub-governors,
Mohammed Abu-Nabbut ('Father of the Cudgel'), a freed slave of
Jazzar, ruled Jaffa with the same tyranny as his master. He built a
mosque at Jaffa, and two fountains, one at the southern entrance to
the town, the other in its centre.

The Christian communities of the Holy Land were subject to many
vexations during the Turkish rule. These included the confiscation
of the Franciscan property of Mount Zion (the Coenaculum and its
vicinity) and the ejection of the monks of the Custodia Terra Santa
from their monastery. The monks were eventually able to build a new
monastery in the Christian quarter of the Old City. The Greek
Orthodox community, whose members were in general subjects of
the Ottoman sultan (the Roman Catholic were French, Italian and
Spanish monks, protected by the Capitulation agreements), enjoyed
the favour of the Turks. When a fire broke out in 1808 beneath
the Rotonda of the Holy Sepulchre, it was the Greek Orthodox
community which was entrusted with the reconstruction of the Sepulchre. The resulting aedicule, in a Turkish rococo style, was the work
of a master-craftsman from Mitylene.

◁
Jerusalem. 16th-century Turkish buildings in the citadel.

*Minaret of the Umariyya Mosque adjoining the church of
the Holy Sepulchre with dome and cross.*

▷

*Minaret of the White Mosque at Ramla, built by
Mameluke Sultan Qalaun (1318).*

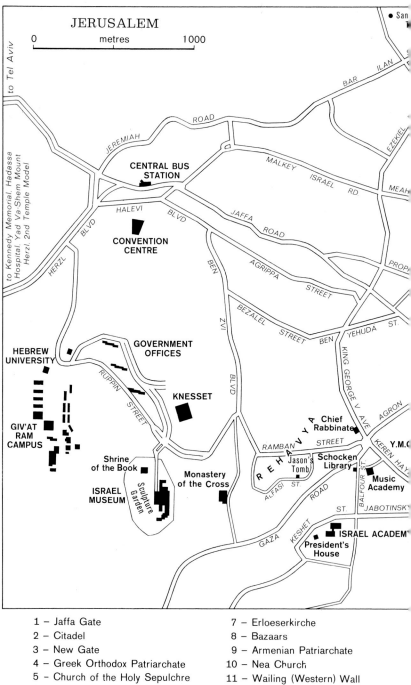

JERUSALEM

0   metres   1000

• San

to Tel Aviv

to Kennedy Memorial, Hadassa Hospital, Yad Va-Shem Mount Herzl, 2nd Temple Model

ILAN

BAR

JEREMIAH

ROAD

EZEKIEL

MALKEY ISRAEL RD

MEAH

CENTRAL BUS STATION

HALEVI

BLVD

HERZL BLVD

JAFFA ROAD

CONVENTION CENTRE

BEN ZVI BLVD

AGRIPPA STREET

PROP

HEBREW UNIVERSITY

RUPPIN STREET

GOVERNMENT OFFICES

BEZALEL STREET

BEN YEHUDA ST.

KING GEORGE V AVE

AGRON

KNESSET

GIV'AT RAM CAMPUS

Chief Rabbinate

Y.M.C

RAMBAN

STREET

KEREN HAY

Shrine of the Book

Monastery of the Cross

R E H A V Y A

Jason's Tomb

Schocken Library

Music Academy

BALFOUR ST.

ISRAEL MUSEUM

Sculpture Garden

ALFASI ST.

ROAD

ST.

JABOTINSK

GAZA

KESHET ROAD

ISRAEL ACADEM

President's House

1 – Jaffa Gate
2 – Citadel
3 – New Gate
4 – Greek Orthodox Patriarchate
5 – Church of the Holy Sepulchre
6 – Russian convent (Alexandrovsky)

7 – Erloeserkirche
8 – Bazaars
9 – Armenian Patriarchate
10 – Nea Church
11 – Wailing (Western) Wall
12 – Islamic Museum

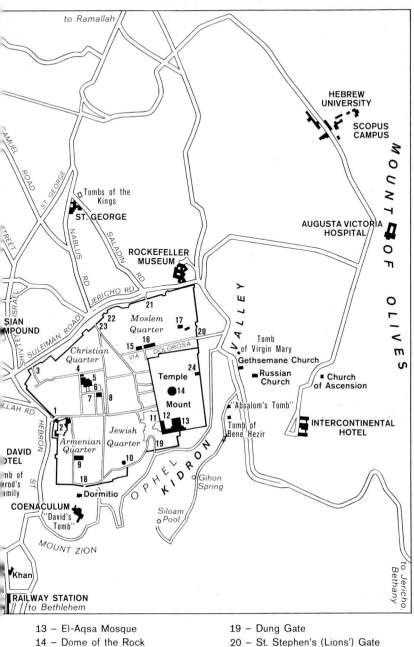

13 – El-Aqsa Mosque
14 – Dome of the Rock
15 – Ecce Homo Arch, Antonia
16 – Flagellatio
17 – St. Anne and Sheep's Pool
18 – Zion Gate

19 – Dung Gate
20 – St. Stephen's (Lions') Gate
21 – Herod's Gate
22 – "Solomon's Quarries"
23 – Damascus Gate
24 – Golden Gate

P. 210/211
Street in Armenian quarter, close to wall.

The Jews fared relatively well under Ottoman rule, until internal security disintegrated in the seventeenth century. Already in Mameluke times some refugees from the persecutions of the Spanish Inquisition found shelter here. In the sixteenth century the Spaniard Don Josef Nassi and his relation Donna Grazia were encouraged by the sultan Suleiman to settle Tiberias and its vicinity with Jews. Although the project for establishing Jewish agricultural communities in Galilee proved premature at that time, the city of Tiberias has remained largely Jewish ever since. Another Jewish centre arose at Safed in Upper Galilee. In the seventeenth century groups of Cabbalists led by Isaac Lurieh (called after his title and initials ARI—Adonenu Rabbenu Isaac, 'our Lord and teacher Isaac'—but Ari also means 'lion' in Hebrew) settled at Safed. Two old synagogues are dedicated to his memory, one of the Sephardic, the other of the Ashkenazi rite. The Sephardic synagogue, which is the older, is entered from a small court. An anteroom leads to the main hall, which is aligned southwards and adjoins a small cave. The synagogue has three windows overlooking the mountain landscape in front of Safed. We are told that ARI himself liked to look at the mountains from this spot. The main hall has two vaults, under one of which stands the *almemar*, or praying podium. The synagogue was first built in the seventeenth century, but it has been reconstructed several times, preserving the original plan. The Ashkenazi synagogue was built several years after the death of ARI. It has richly decorated windows over the main entrance, and contains a wooden Ark of the Covenant, the masterpiece of an artist woodworker from Kolomea in Galicia. The Ark is made in the style of woodwork evolved among the Jews of Eastern Europe, with a complicated open-scroll decoration. An outstanding detail is the mythical fish or dragon from whose mouth issue flame-coloured streamers which twist between the floral ornaments.

The Jews of Safed were not, however, entirely plunged in the mystic depths of the Cabbala. They were busy with textile and other industries, and even enjoyed the privilege of setting up in the city the first printing press ever to work in the Holy Land. Rabbinical learning also flourished in their midst. One of the rabbis of Safed in the sixteenth century was the celebrated Josef Caro, whose code of orthodox Jewish practice, the *Shulkhan Arukh* ('well-ordered table') is still the standard work on the subject with the addition of the *Mappa* ('tablecloth') provided by Rabbi Isserles of Cracow.

The Nineteenth Century and the Mandatory Period

The Napoleonic campaign in Egypt and Palestine (1799) ended in failure; it marks nevertheless a turning point in the history of Palestine. The country had hitherto, for all the influx of pilgrims, merchants and travellers, lain outside the orbit of western culture, with the dead hand

▷

Acre. Khan-el-Franj. One of the caravanserais built for the convenience of European merchants.

P. 214/215

Acre. Mosque of Ahmad Pasha el-Jazzar. The mosque is surrounded by domed cells for students of Muslim theology. The dome and slender minaret reproduce the style of the imperial mosques of Istanbul.

of Ottoman pashadom weighing upon it. Now the Orient, and first of all its rulers, became aware of the superiority—especially in the matter of warfare—of the European *homo technicus*. This lesson was first learnt in Egypt where Napoleon had made his initial impact. The Albanian rulers of this country, Muhammad Ali and his son Ibrahim, profited from the European methods when wresting Palestine from Turkish rule. Even Acre, which had defied Napoleon, fell to Ibrahim Pasha. For ten years (1831-41) the country was administered with a semblance of European order. But even after the reinforcement of its walls Acre could not resist an attack in 1840 by an Anglo-Austrian squadron, and Ibrahim was forced to evacuate the Holy Land and restore it to the Turks. Yet the manner of the restoration of Ottoman rule proved in itself once more the superiority of the West. The Turks who returned in 1841 were forced to adopt many of the administrative methods of the Europeans. The capitulatory regime, which was designed to safeguard the 'Frankish' merchants cooped up in a commercial ghetto, now served to protect the activities of European missionaries, merchants and scholars. The intervention of the consuls of the European powers, each much stronger than the 'sick man of Europe', was feared by the central and local Turkish administrations.

The return to Western influences—the first since the end of the Byzantine period, apart from the episode of the Crusades—was marked by the rivalry of the great powers, a rivalry mainly expressed in religious terms. Russia, one of the chief rivals, became the patron of the Greek Orthodox community. Thousands of pilgrims were coming from the Tsarist empire. Accommodation was provided for them in the hospices built at Jerusalem and Nazareth, around churches with the typical bulb-shaped domes of Russian architecture. To this day the monuments of a pious Russian past can be seen in the 'Russian Compound' at Jerusalem, and in the church at Gethsemane. Russia's principal rival was Catholic France. Massive buildings, of the style associated with French ecclesiastic architecture of the nineteenth century, dotted the landscape at Jerusalem (Notre Dame), Emmaus, Jaffa, etc. The rivalry of the two powers led to the Crimean War, which was ostensibly sparked off in the grotto of the Church of the Nativity at Bethlehem when the silver star with its Latin inscription was surreptitiously removed by Orthodox monks.

The other European powers, Germany, Austria and Italy, each acted on its own. Germany had the double advantage of representing both Catholic and Protestant interests. The Italian hospital in Jerusalem imitates a Florentine palace. The massive Victoria-Augusta Hospital on the Mount of Olives is unmistakably in the style of Wilhelm's Prussia. The German Protestants made a still more significant contribution to the local landscape by establishing garden suburbs near Jerusalem, Haifa and Jaffa, and agricultural colonies at Wilhelma and Bethlehem in Galilee. These neat villages, with their red roofs and well-tended gardens, were maintained by the Templars. These Protestant communities showed what ingenuity and diligence could achieve in a country apparently still mostly a desert. The laying of the railway line to Jerusalem, and the linking of the Hejaz railway with Haifa, marked the beginning of modern methods of communication in the Holy Land.

◁
Sea wall at Acre.

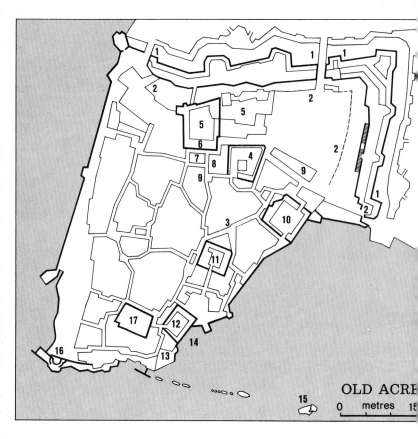

1 – Jazzar's Wall, fosse and counterscarp
2 – Gate
3 – Bazaar
4 – Jazzar's mosque and tomb
5 – Citadel
6 – Refectory of St John
7 – Ḥammam el-Basha (Museum)
8 – El Bosta
9 – Turkish bazaar
10 – Khan esh-Shawarda
11 – Khan el Franj
12 – Khan el Umdan
13 – Sea gate
14 – Harbour
15 – Tower of Flies and ancient ṃ
16 – Lighthouse
17 – Khan esh Shuna

OLD ACRE

The nineteenth century also saw the beginning of the scientific, topo-graphical and archaeological exploration of Palestine. Here the first in the field was the British Palestine Exploration Fund. It had the country mapped out with scientific precision in the years 1874-77. Other nations followed: the American, Edward Robinson, the French-man, Clermont-Ganneau, and the German, Conrad Schick, travelled all over Palestine and surveyed the remains of its past, identifying the biblical sites as they went. The archaeological excavations which sup-ply the bulk of the knowledge summarized in the preceding pages began in the nineteenth century. De Saulcy worked at the Tombs of the Kings in Jerusalem (1864). It was the revolutionary idea of Flinders Petrie at Tell el Hesi, that the humble potsherds were the key to the chronology of the ancient sites, which entirely transformed the study of the remains of the past.

Old city of Jaffa, now largely restored.

The gradual westernization of Palestine continued until the end of Ottoman rule in 1918. After the upheaval caused by the fighting in the First World War Palestine became a British Mandate. For the next thirty years it was administered by a High Commissioner appointed by London, assisted by British civil servants in leading positions. The new administration created the foundations of a modern state, but its activities were inhibited by the political conflict between the obligation imposed on it to assist in the establishment of a 'Jewish national home', and Arab nationalism which had flourished on the ruins of the Ottoman empire. For all its endeavours the British administration has not left many lasting monuments. In Jerusalem the British built a palace for their High Commissioner (Government House), and the Rockefeller Museum, both by A. Harrison in a semi-Oriental style, eclectic in nature and distinguished only by the artistic ability of the architect. Other buildings of the Mandate period were the post offices at Jerusalem and Jaffa (the former marked by a tasteful use of alternate layers of white and black stone) and the Haifa Municipality. Among the buildings attributable to ecclesiastical initiative in that period

are the Church of St Andrew and the Bible House in Jerusalem (both by Clifford Holiday). The Jerusalem Municipality and Barclay's Bank were less successful examples in the same style. The eclectic style of Italian church construction is exemplified by the Gethsemane church with its overladen façade.

The tomb of the founder of the Bahai sect, built in Haifa in a spacious garden, represents, with its gilt cupola and white marble walls, a continuation of this Oriental tradition, although it was erected when the modern architectural vogue was already in full swing.

Another type of monument with which the Mandatory Government saddled the country was a series of police stations, the so-called 'Teggart fortresses' which cover the country: huge and costly blocks of concrete, which in the end could neither prevent the Arab rising nor save the Mandate in the hour of its crisis.

Public fountain built on the outskirts of Jaffa by Abu Nabbut ('Father of the Cudgel'), former slave and governor on behalf of Jazzar.

◁
Old Synagogue, Safed.

P. 222/223
Russian church, Gethsemane.

Jewish Immigration - the State of Israel

Diverse civilizations have successively left many traces for the visitor to the Holy Land. But essentially he will be faced with a living country, where the present, if not indeed a hint of the future, will assume before his eyes a proportion that will certainly not fail to surprise him. A great multitude of Jewish immigrants, a flood from the four corners of the earth, has fused itself into a new demographic and cultural entity, into a society which, despite the special conditions of its birth and evolution, appears to resemble any other society of the technological and industrial era.

The stages of this effort to adapt to new ways or life, evolving in response to circumstances often unforeseen and almost always dramatic, have spanned less than a century. But this century already has its history, its past, even its own traces left: in its beginnings—which go back to the last days of the Ottoman Empire—the idea prevailed of a return to the Promised Land, an idea that impelled several thousand emancipated young people to leave the confines of their eastern European ghettos. 1878 saw the foundation of the first agricultural settlement, Petah-Tiqva, today a town of 100,000 people in the suburbs of Tel Aviv. Until that time the native Jewish population had been gathered in the small communities that had persisted for several hundred years in the four traditionally holy cities of Jerusalem, Hebron, Safed and Tiberias. After 1870 there came into being, one by one, the Agricultural School of Mikve Israel near Jaffa, and the villages of Zikhron Ya'aqov on Mount Carmel and Rehovot and Rishon le Zion south of the old Jaffa-Jerusalem road. It was not only a return to the Promised Land, but more simply a return to the land itself, a symbolic return to vine, corn and orange.

A few old houses still remain in these villages. Massive rectangular one-storey buildings of local stone, often surrounded by venerable cypresses, stand solidly in the centre of Zikhron Ya'aqov, and not far away in the single street of the village of Bat Shelomo. In the narrow alleys beside the main street, in Rehovot, Rishon le Zion and Mazkeret Batya, another kind of house is still to be found, with a large projecting balcony at the front, beneath a wooden roof. Further south at Gedera, the curious neo-classical decoration on the town hall recalls the 1890s. All these give evidence of the work of technicians sent to Palestine by Baron Edmond de Rothschild, whose financial and technical support enabled the first villages to be built and developed.

Another version of the Return, which preceded the advent of political

▷

Bahai shrine. Haifa.

View of Jerusalem from Mount of Olives, *1858, by Edward Lear (1813-88).*
Pen and watercolour. Israel Museum.

Zionism in 1897, found expression in the extremely curious planning
of Meah Shearim, the old religious quarter of Jerusalem. This too
dates from the end of the last century. It is in fact a ghetto, or rather
a succession of ghettos, transplanted from central and eastern Europe
into the Levant: its triangular court, surrounded by religious schools
and synagogues, is inward-looking and cut off from the modern town.
Meah Shearim's street, with its long, severe buildings called 'Warsaw
Houses', or 'Hungarian Houses', bears witness to the origins of the
population. So do those fur hats and black velvet coats worn by
young and old orthodox Jews in the manner of Polish and Hungarian
noblemen in the seventeenth century.
That this closed, changeless community should exist is in no way
unusual; this can be confirmed no more than a few hundred yards

away, inside the precincts of the Old City. Muslim, Christian, Armenian and Jewish quarters each have an entity, and each is characterized by its own way of life. The tireless repetition of the stone, the tiny courtyards hidden behind imposing porches, arches and cupolas, the ceaseless coming and going of the traders and the tourists—these create the harmony und unity of the town, and link the quarters one with another; but they also emphasize the permanence of forms and of ways of life and thought that belong to the Near East of the Middle Ages.

P. 228/229
Tel Aviv Museum.

Ein Karem, *1944, by Mordecai Ardon. Oil on canvas. Israel Museum.*

Other kinds of dwelling and ways of living are traditionally typical of Arab towns and villages. The old *souks* of Jerusalem, swarming with life from dawn to dusk, have their lesser counterparts at Acre, Nablus, Bethlehem and Nazareth. Residential areas have grown up around these *souks* whose severe stone often plays a decorative part, picking out the shape of a window or forming a curve above a door. But Jaffa, some thousands of years old, is very different: on the hill overlooking the ancient port, Arab, Turk and Italian have cleverly

▷

King David playing the harp. *From Rothschild Manuscript 24, Ferrara, Italy. Detail from a page from an illuminated miscellany containing over 50 religious and secular works by at least three anonymous artists. Israel Museum.*

אָשְׁרֵי

הָאִישׁ אֲשֶׁר לֹא הָלַךְ בַּעֲצַת רְשָׁעִים וּבְדֶרֶךְ חַטָּאִים לֹא עָ׳
עָמָד וּבְמוֹשַׁב לֵצִים לֹא יָשָׁב: כִּי אִם בְּתוֹרַת יְהֹוָה חֶפְצוֹ וּבְ
וּבְתוֹרָתוֹ יֶהְגֶּה יוֹמָם וָלָיְלָה: וְהָיָה כְּעֵץ שָׁתוּל עַל פַּלְגֵי מַיִם
אֲשֶׁר פִּרְיוֹ יִתֵּן בְּעִתּוֹ וְעָלֵהוּ לֹא יִבּוֹל וְכֹל אֲשֶׁר יַעֲשֶׂה יַצְלִ
יַצְלִיחַ: לֹא כֵן הָרְשָׁעִים כִּי אִם כַּמֹּץ אֲשֶׁר תִּדְּפֶנּוּ רוּחַ: עַל
כֵּן לֹא יָקֻמוּ רְשָׁעִים בַּמִּשְׁפָּט וְחַטָּאִים בַּעֲדַת צַדִּיקִים
כִּי יוֹדֵעַ יְהֹוָה דֶּרֶךְ צַדִּיקִים וְדֶרֶךְ רְשָׁעִים תֹּאבֵד:
לָמָּה רָגְשׁוּ גוֹיִם וּלְאֻמִּים יֶהְגּוּ רִיק: יִתְיַצְּבוּ
מַלְכֵי אֶרֶץ וְרוֹזְנִים נוֹסְדוּ יָחַד עַל יְהֹוָה וְעַל מְשִׁיחוֹ: נְנַתְּקָה
נְנַתְּקָה אֶת מוֹסְרוֹתֵימוֹ וְנַשְׁלִיכָה מִמֶּנּוּ עֲבֹתֵימוֹ: יוֹשֵׁב
בַּשָּׁמַיִם יִשְׂחָק יְהֹוָה יִלְעַג לָמוֹ: אָז יְדַבֵּר אֵלֵימוֹ בְאַפּוֹ וּבַחֲרוֹ
וּבַחֲרוֹנוֹ יְבַהֲלֵמוֹ: וַאֲנִי נָסַכְתִּי מַלְכִּי עַל צִיּוֹן הַר קָדְשִׁי: אֲ
אֲסַפְּרָה אֶל חֹק יְהֹוָה אָמַר אֵלַי בְּנִי אַתָּה אֲנִי הַיּוֹם יְלִדְתִּיךָ
שְׁאַל מִמֶּנִּי וְאֶתְּנָה גוֹיִם נַחֲלָתֶךָ וַאֲחֻזָּתְךָ אַפְסֵי אָרֶץ: תְּ
תְּרֹעֵם בְּשֵׁבֶט בַּרְזֶל כִּכְלִי יוֹצֵר תְּנַפְּצֵם: וְעַתָּה מְלָכִים הַשְׂ

vied with one another to build houses that lean upon each other, with little wooden balconies overhanging the alleyways, and little flights of steps, which add a special flavour to every detail of the scene. Also two basic types of Arab village can be distinguished: those in the mountains of Judaea, Samaria and Galilee, huddled on the hillsides, clinging to every least topographical advantage in the terraced rock; and those down in the lower hills, barely lifted above the plain, with houses coloured turquoise and pale blue.

There is a sharp contrast between these traditional towns and villages, and the organized confusion of the Jewish towns and villages. This is first of all a contrast between ways of living that echo and perpetuate the ancient East, borrowing from the West only what is essential to their own full development; and the entirely occidental urge to create a town or village through the medium of a plan, attempting to manage and direct its evolution. It is a contrast between the town patiently built up by the whole community, and the town of the architects and planners. It is also the contrast between the historical site, brought to the fore by historic imperatives, and the site chosen on administrative or economic grounds. Finally it is the contrast between the East of mountains and sunshine that obliges the villages to depend upon the small market towns, and the West with its dynamism on a larger scale, its goal the conversion of non-civilized areas.

This profound transformation of the country has been the result of the advent of political Zionism and of the pogroms in eastern Europe. After 1900 the immigrants no longer arrived in small parties but in their thousands. And the formation of the first kibbutzim in the north of the country symbolized, far more than the earlier creation of the first agricultural villages, a new approach to life. It also marked the beginning of town-planning and architecture that were no longer anonymous. The kibbutz itself is a symbol, in which man can conceive his future existence from a beginning. The kibbutz is swampy ground, arid land or prairie transformed into a settlement. A rural prototype comes into being, making possible the division of labour, the planning and construction of residential accommodation and common services around the community centre that contains the dining-room, schools, reading and lecture rooms. The solutions adopted are reminiscent of the methods of the German Bauhaus. The moshav, or collective village, used the kibbutz system and adapted it to its own needs. Its capacity for rational organization is best exemplified at Nahalal, a circular moshav built to the design of the architect, Richard Kaufmann, around 1920.

It is not enough to see the kibbutzim to assess the magnitude of the effort applied to the transformation of nature. One must go south, to Beersheba, to the new town of Arad—the last human presence before the dramatic descent to the Dead Sea—to Dimona, a town of recent immigrants—Moroccans, Persians, but also Jews from Africa and Bedouins. The desert rings the town as the forest used to surround the old towns of Europe. The trees, the plants, the cornfields and cottonfields lie scattered in big squares across a seemingly endless landscape. In all the southern half of the country civilization is culture, in the strictest sense of the word. And the time of men is measured by the height of the trees, or by the whiteness of the houses.

◁
Tel Aviv.

Tel Aviv. Bauhaus architecture. Workers' flats: architect, Arieh Sharon (above).

▷

Modern architecture in Tel Aviv (above right); in Beersheba (below right).

Haifa. Rothschild House, Mount Carmel Theatre: architect, A. Mansfeld (below).

*Jerusalem. Israel Museum, interior (above) and exterior (below):
architects, A. Mansfeld and D. Gad.*

Kennedy Memorial near Jerusalem: architect, D. Reznik.

This effort is likewise to be observed in the three large towns of the country, Tel Aviv, Jerusalem and Haifa. Tel Aviv was founded in 1909, and is today a town of 400,000 inhabitants and the cultural centre of the Jewish population. Its appearance, its cultural institutions, its development and the intensity of its life would in themselves be sufficient evidence of the rapid growth of the Jewish population in Palestine and the way in which a mass of immigrants transformed themselves into a cultural entity.

The waves of immigration began, as we have seen, in the last years of the nineteenth century. A second movement followed the Russian Revolution of 1905. The immigrants, mostly from Russia and Poland, founded villages and kibbutzim or settled in Jerusalem or Jaffa. Initially Tel Aviv was no more than a small residential suburb developed on the outskirts of Jaffa. Its impetus for rapid growth was provided by the third wave of immigration that followed the first world war and the setting up of the British Mandate. Before 1930 the population had risen to 50,000. The first Jewish theatres were built here, Herzliya—the first secondary school—was founded here, and newspaper offices were transferred here from Jerusalem. Prominent in this Renaissance figured the Hebrew language, which had been in virtual oblivion for two thousand years.

The 'old' centre of Tel Aviv still shows what the town was like before 1930: Geulah, Nahlat-Benyamin and Herzl Street, nowadays shopping centres, were originally the main arteries serving the first residential areas of a modest suburb. Their one- and two-storey houses display a curious mixture of styles typical of Eastern Europe and fanciful variations on local oriental themes. Cupolas and triangular-arched windows are overshadowed by Migdal Shalom, the first skyscraper built forty years later.

A fourth wave of immigration brought 60,000 Jews from Germany and central Europe, in flight from the Nazi regime after 1933. Again the appearance of the town altered. In Ahad-Ha'am and Bialik Streets, and around Dizengoff Street, there arose buildings unequivocally modern in design, recalling the German Bauhaus in purity of line and

Ramat-Gan, Dubiner House: architects, Z. Hecker, A. Neumann and E. Sharon.

rejection of the accessory decorative effects of Art Nouveau. Their presence in Tel Aviv is a real curiosity. They include the old museum, opened in 1933 and recently transferred to new premises, and the workers' flats in Frug Street, the work of a former student of the Bauhaus, architect Arieh Sharon. Other remarkable buildings along the same lines were by the famous German-Jewish architect Erich Mendelssohn in Jerusalem: the office of the Leumi Bank (1937), the Schocken Library (1935)—home of an important collection of Jewish illuminated books and manuscripts from the Middle Ages—and the old Hadassah Hospital on Mount Scopus (1936).

A more romantic approach can be recognized in the architecture of several public buildings put up before the second world war. We have already mentioned the Rockefeller Museum and the Residence of the British High Commissioner, both designed by English architects. The Jerusalem YMCA is also interesting. Like the Sacré Coeur in Paris or the Rockefeller Center in New York, they refer back to the past to produce an expression of monumental dignity. Here it is a sort of Byzantinesque effect which is produced, eclectic but nevertheless conscious of the qualities of the local stone.

The state of Israel, founded in 1948, received more than a million and a half immigrants, mostly refugees from Europe, North Africa and the Near East. The country's population more than doubled. It was the start of a new era for town-planning and architecture. First, a renewed extension of Tel Aviv and of the satellites mushrooming around it, Ramat-Gan, Holon, Bat-Yam. But, more important, new towns were created, along general lines inspired by British post-war town-planning: residential areas built about shopping and community centres, and accumulating one upon another to make up a whole not only well defined but capable of further extension. The towns of Beersheba, Kiryat-Gat, Dimona and Arad, and more recently the port of Ashdod, are in this class. They all lie in the southern half of the country which was until recently almost uninhabited.

During the first years that followed the founding of the state of Israel, few buildings of any great interest were put up. About 1955, as the pace of immigration began to decline, attention began to focus, little by little, on the quality of public buildings. The influence of the Bauhaus, evident in Leopold Krakauer's dining-rooms for the kibbutzim of Beth Alpha and Tel-Yosef, gave place to the ideas of Le Corbusier, and in general to the so-called international style. This new trend is visible in the new residential blocks on the way into Beersheba (architects: Yaski and Alexandroni), in the headquarters of the Histadrut—the Labour Federation—at Tel Aviv (architect: D. Carmi), and at the Hebrew University in Jerusalem, particularly in its administrative buildings by D. Carmi and the National and University Library, which is the work of a group of architects.

The years after 1955 saw more original designs. On the campus of the Hebrew University the students' synagogue was built by Heinz Rau and David Reznik. It is in the form of a dome that covers a

▷

Mosaic wall of Beit-Hahayal (Soldier's House) 9 m. high, by Avigdor Arikha (b. 1929), Jerusalem.

P. 242/243

Safed, c. 1924, by Yosef Zaritsky. Watercolour. An early work by one of the leaders of the Abstract Movement in Israel. Israel Museum.

windowless storey, taking its light all around from the ground floor. Also in Jerusalem is the Yad Va-Shem Memorial, the work of Arieh Elhanani, the striking austerity of its square mass enhanced by the use of heavy black basalt blocks topped by a reinforced concrete roof. The Israel Museum in Jerusalem, opened in May 1965, is by Al Mansfeld and Dora Gad. It is a vast complex of pavilions, and develops as a series of variations on a square module, layered like an Arab village along the contours of the hill. The Billy Rose Garden of Art (sculptures by Rodin, Maillol, Bourdelle, Picasso, Moore, Vasarély, Tinguely, etc.), which is a part of the museum, was designed by Isamu Noguchi, the American sculptor and landscape architect. It consists of five semi-circular terraces in local stone, overlooking the hills that surround the city. The Shrine of the Book completes the Israel Museum, and houses a part of the Dead Sea Scrolls and other objects dating from the second revolt against the Romans in 132 AD. Its architects, the Americans Bartos and Kiesler, have given it a symbolic aspect—the white dome refers to the Sect of the Sons of Light, and the black wall to that of the Sons of Darkness. Also in Jerusalem is David Reznik's Soldier's House whose pure but impressive lines are almost those of a fortress.

So Jerusalem, city of splendid monuments from the past, is becoming changed and enriched by new structures that bear witness to its present vitality and to the administrative and cultural functions it has been called upon to assume. The architecture of Tel Aviv has been governed by very different imperatives. Demographic pressures, industrialization, and purely economic factors have been the causes for high-rise construction and the destruction of the traditional proportions of the 1930s. The first of these blocks, the El Al Building, designed by D. Carmi, is still in the international style. The Hilton Hotel, built about 1965 by Yaakov Rechter, is more concerned with the landscape and the light as it half-turns its balconies towards the sea. Another elegant and harmonious achievement is the new Tel Aviv Museum, by Isaac Yashar and Dan Eytan, opened in 1971. Its deliberately modest exterior encloses large and spacious exhibition rooms that make circulation easy and are marvellously illuminated. The Fredric Mann Auditorium (architects: D. Carmi and Meltzer) is one of the largest and most modern concert halls in the world, and forms part of a cultural complex that also includes the two auditoriums of the Habimah National Theatre.

The buildings described above are mostly by architects from Europe. They have been the pioneers of a modern Israeli architecture. Other younger men have been trained at the Haifa Technion. Two of these, Zvi Hecker and Eldad Sharon, were originally pupils and collaborators of Alfred Neumann, who refined the principles of a 'morphological' architecture at the Technion. These theories are applied in two buildings by this group, the town hall at Bat-Yam and the Dubiner Building at Ramat-Gan, two towns in the suburbs of Tel Aviv. Both are worked out to a formal system in which the units or elements of the construction are like variations on the basic theme of a complex geometrical module. Thus the Bat-Yam town hall is in the form of an 'inverted pyramid' carrying in its roof 'mouths of

◁

Menashe Kadishman, sculpture, Tension 1966 *in the Billy Rose Garden, Israel Museum, Jerusalem.*

light' rather like sculptures, with a play upon the tetrahedron motif. The Dubiner Building recalls Habitat in Montreal—which it pre-dates— with its set of superimposed apartments making up a sort of huge fantastic sculpture. The Faculty of Mechanical Engineering, by Hecker and Neumann, is also a fine example of this 'morphological' architecture. The Denmark School, the work of two young architects, Dan and Ilana Alrod, shows another facet of Israeli architecture today, the attempt to adapt modern structures to the very spirit of the landscape, using the contours of the ground and grouping the various units in relation to the environment.

The plastic arts in Israel may be said to be relative newcomers. Their history is contemporary with Zionism and dates back, therefore, no further than the turn of the century. In the Western sense of the term, all artistic creation until that time had to do with the forms and techniques of oriental craftsmanship. There were indeed Jewish artists in Safed, Tiberias and Jerusalem, whose occasional representations of biblical or religious scenes on paper or glass are still preserved, many in the Israel Museum. But the true advent of painting and sculpture was really the work of a group of immigrants who founded a School of Art in Jerusalem in 1906. It was known as Bezalel, after the name of the first 'artist' mentioned in the Bible. Its founder, Boris Schatz, and his disciples came originally from Eastern Europe, and their work was heavily imbued with Art Nouveau and romantic naturalism. After the first world war it was their pupils who evolved a sort of local School. One of them, the sculptor Melnikov, created the 'Lion' of Tel-Hay in Upper Galilee, the country's first 'monument'. This school, whose activities carried on almost until the second world war, was very much influenced by Cézanne, by the French Intimists, and above all by the Jewish Expressionist painters of the Paris School. It was only after 1945 that Palestinian art emerged from a long isolation, exposing itself to the influences of the French and American post-war schools. The 'New Horizons' group—founded by Marcel Janco, a

◁
The Lake of Tiberias, *1923, by Reuven Rubin. Oil on canvas.*
This work is characteristic of the idealist and primitive work of the
first generation of Palestine artists. Israel Museum.

The High Commissioner, *1966, by Arieh Aroch. Oil on wood. Israel Museum*

◁
Observation Post, *Arad,
detail, by Ygael Tumarkin.*

*Modern cairns by shore of
Dead Sea by Doron Bar-Adon.*

former Dadaist group member from Zurich who emigrated to Palestine in 1941, and by Yosef Zaritsky, who had come from his native Russia in 1923, and whose remarkable landscapes had been evolving towards abstraction throughout the 1930s—was largely instrumental in bringing about this opening-up towards the outside world. Under Zaritsky's influence, local art outstepped its self-imposed constraints, transforming various formulae of free abstraction into an idiom in which expression is often more important than form. Janco was also the founder of the artists' village of Ein Hod near Haifa, where artists and craftsmen work together. Another painter, Mordecai Ardon, both through his art and by his teaching, influenced young artists who were later to explore more formal approaches. He was a former pupil of Klee and Feininger at the Bauhaus, and his work brings together abstract elements in a context that seeks chiefly to be symbolic, and refers essentially to the drama of the Jewish people under the Nazi regime. His *Triptych*, in the Israel Museum, is typical of his style.

Bazaar scene in Jerusalem.

The first truly Israeli generation, which is to say the artists who have grown up with the state of Israel, is not so very different from its young European or American counterpart. A variety of trends, ranging from abstraction to new figurative art, from representational art grounded in the Jewish tradition to frankly experimental research work, is represented in the collections of the Israel Museum and the Tel Aviv Museum. But the trends are also apparent in the form of reliefs, mosaics, sculptures and monuments in buildings and public places. The most outstanding examples deserve mention.

Several works are representative of the evolution of Yakov Agam, an Israeli living in Paris, where he was one of the pioneers of kinetic art: the relief on the ceiling of the Convention Hall (Binyanei Haooma) in Jerusalem, a large sculpture in the Israel Museum and a recent relief (1970) in the Tel Aviv Museum. Avigdor Arikha's quality of profound spirituality expressed in an essentially abstract idiom can be adjudged from several paintings in the Israel Museum and a remarkable

mosaic wall on the patio of the Soldier's House in Jerusalem. Sculptures by Yigael Tumarkin, in the new seaport town of Ashdod, on the way into Dimona, and including *Observation Post* at Arad, convey a sense of space, light and shade, if not even of a strange presence, through a combination of abstract and symbolic elements. *Observation Post*, a concrete monument sited in a grandiose, almost lunar landscape, is the most complete and significant of Tumarkin's works. Mention should also be made of David Palombo's iron *Doors* at the Yad Va-Shem Memorial and at the Knesset (parliament), both in Jerusalem, executed in an abstract idiom at once expressive and austere. The same qualities of dignity and austerity characterize D. Karavan's *Wall*, in the Assembly chamber of the Knesset.

The presence of works by foreign artists—other than in museum collections—is a relatively recent phenomenon in Israel, and one that shows how the development of architecture and town-planning is accompanied by a certain need to 'personalize' public buildings and places. And in the museums themselves, besides the Billy Rose Garden of Art already described, there is the unique set of 130 small works by Jacques Lipchitz, a really comprehensive retrospective of variations upon the principal themes of his work; paintings by the Impressionist masters, Picasso, Braque (in particular a Fauve Braque), European and American post-war artists. In the Tel Aviv Museum, James Ensor's *Favourite Room*, painted reliefs by Archipenko, and a big Henry Moore bronze all form part of a collection of contemporary artists which is continually being enlarged. Outside the museums, there are several important works by modern masters to be found in Jerusalem, including Chagall's well-known stained glass windows in the synagogue of the Hadassah Medical Centre, representing the twelve prophets. In the Knesset there are tapestries making up a triptych (1965-68), whose panels portray respectively *Exodus, Creation,* and *Entry into Jerusalem*. In the very centre of the town Jean Arp's *Three Graces* was set up in King George Street in 1971.

▷

Rosh ha-Niqrah (Ladder of Tyre). General view of coastal rocks and cable car to caves.

P. 254/255.
Old City of Jerusalem from the Jericho Road.

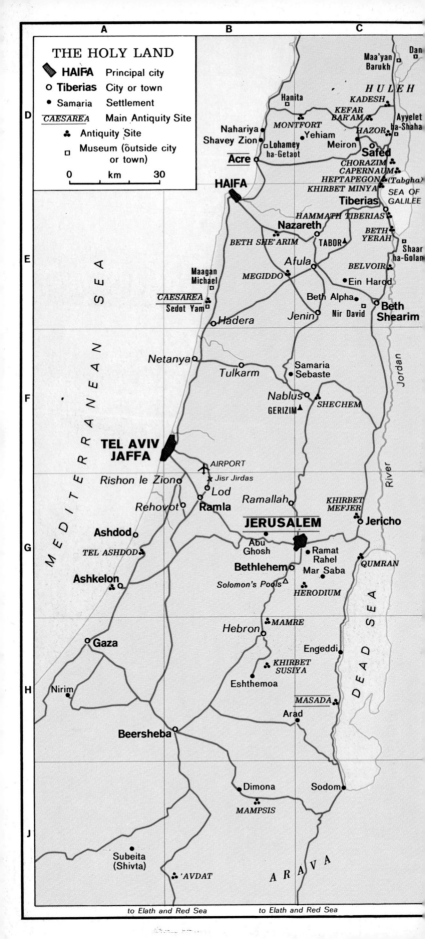

THE HOLY LAND

HAIFA Principal city
○ Tiberias City or town
● Samaria Settlement
CAESAREA Main Antiquity Site
♣ Antiquity Site
□ Museum (outside city or town)

0   km   30

MEDITERRANEAN SEA

D

Dan
Maa'yan Barukh
HULEH
KADESH
Hanita
KEFAR BAR'AM
MONTFORT
Nahariya
Shavey Zion
Yehiam
HAZOR
Ayyelet ha-Shaha
Lohamey ha-Getaot
Meiron
Safed
Acre
CHORAZIM
CAPERNAUM
HEPTAPEGON (Tabgha)
KHIRBET MINYA
HAIFA
Tiberias
SEA OF GALILEE
Nazareth
HAMMATH TIBERIAS
BETH SHE'ARIM
TABOR
BETH YERAH
MEGIDDO
Afula
Shaar ha-Golan

E

Maagan Michael
CAESAREA
Sedot Yam
BELVOIR
Ein Harod
Beth Alpha
Nir David
Beth Shearim
Hadera
Jenin

Netanya
Tulkarm
Samaria
Sebaste

Jordan River

F

Nablus
GERIZIM
SHECHEM

TEL AVIV JAFFA
AIRPORT
Rishon le Zion
Jisr Jirdas
Lod
Rehovot
Ramla
Ramallah
KHIRBET MEFJER
○ Jericho

G

Ashdod
TEL ASHDOD
JERUSALEM
Abu Ghosh
Ramat Rahel
Mar Saba
QUMRAN
Bethlehem
Solomon's Pools
HERODIUM
Ashkelon

DEAD SEA

Hebron
MAMRE
Engeddi

Gaza
KHIRBET SUSIYA

H

Nirim
Eshthemoa
MASADA
Arad

Beersheba

Dimona
Sodom
MAMPSIS

J

Subeita (Shivta)
'AVDAT
ARAVA

to Elath and Red Sea   to Elath and Red Sea

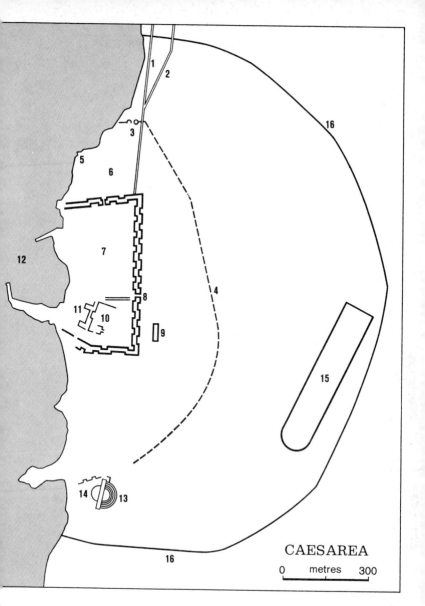

1 – High level aqueduct
2 – Low level aqueduct
3 – Herodian gate towers
4 – Presumed line of Herod's Wall
5 – Site of Synagogue
6 – Site of Straton's Tower
7 – Crusader town, wall and fosse
8 – Crusader gate
9 – Byzantine street, Roman statues
10 – Podium with remains of Byzantine and Crusader churches
11 – Ancient harbour and moles (sanded up)
12 – Underwater remains
13 – Theatre
14 – Byzantine fortress
15 – Hippodrome
16 – Late Roman wall

CAESAREA

0   metres   300

Museums and Galleries

Most museums are open from Sunday to Friday noon (weekdays) and shut on Friday afternoon and Saturday (the Sabbath).

ACRE [DB]
Municipal Museum
Old City. Winter 9–5; summer 9–6; Friday 9–2; eve of holidays 9–12.
Founded in 1954, building once served as a Turkish bath (Hammam el-Basha) of the 18th century. The collection includes archaeological finds from the Canaanite to the Turkish period, glass, pottery (Rhodian jar handles), Crusader reliefs and sculptures. There is also a collection of Persian glazed vessels from the Middle Ages and a collection of arms and armour including Crusader chain-mail and swords. The ethnological collection contains dioramas of Arab and Druze village life, working tools, jewelry, popular art from the Turkish period: textiles, pottery, reliefs in wood.

AYYELET HA-SHAHAR [DC]
Hazor Museum
Founded in 1966 by Ayala and Sam Sachs. Architect: D. Reznik. Finds from Hazor from the Middle Bronze to the Israelite period: pottery, weapons, seals, scarabs, cultic objects, ivory reliefs and figurines.

BEERSHEBA [HB]
Negev Museum
Weekdays 8–7; Friday 8–1; Saturday 10–1.
Founded by the Municipality in the old mosque, 1953. Contains archaeological finds from the site of Beersheba and its vicinity, Chalcolithic remains from es Safadi and Tel Matar, finds from Israelite tombs, including Astarte figurines, fragments of Byzantine church mosiacs, Roman and Byzantine glass. Ethnological collection illustrating Bedouin life. Documents and maps for the history of new Beersheba.

BETH SHEAN [EC]
Municipal Museum
Weekdays 8–3.30; Friday 8–1; Saturday and holidays 10–1.
Founded in 1958 in the former mosque Jami el 'Arbain el-Ghazzawi (*c.* 1800) on 1 D Street. Archaeological finds from Beth Shean and its vicinity, including working tools from the Mesolithic period onwards, ritual synagogue objects, fragments of mosaics of the Roman and Byzantine periods.

DAN [DC]
Ussishkin House
Winter 9–12, 2–4; summer 9–12, 2–5; Friday and eve of holidays 9–12.
Founded in 1958. Architect: L. Krakauer. Collection illustrating natural history of the Huleh Valley; includes archaeological collection of objects found in the region or excavated at Tel Dan.

EIN HAROD [EC]
Art Centre (Mishkan le-Omanut)
Every day 9–12, 3–5.
Founded in 1938 by the painter Haim Attar, who was a member of the kibbutz. The architect of the present building was S. Bickeles. The museum is meant to give a representative view of Jewish art in the Diaspora. Over 1,000 works of art, including paintings by Israels, Liebermann, M. Gottlieb, Y. Adler, the school of Paris, Pascin, Mané-Katz, Kisling, J. Adler, and of Jewish painters of America (R. and M. Soyer, Weber, Lozowick, Kaufmann), and Israel contemporary painters. Over 300 sculptures, 8,000 works of graphic art, Jewish popular art.

Maritime Museum
Weekdays 9–12, 3–5; Saturday, holidays and holiday eves 9–12.
Founded 1950 by Jeremiah Halperin. Aquarium and museum of marine fauna and flora of the Red Sea.

Sturman House
Weekdays 8–4; Friday and holiday eves 8–2; Saturday and holidays 9–12.
Founded in 1941 in memory of Haim Sturman, a pioneer settler in the Jezreel Valley. Architect: D. Laskov. History of the Beth Shean Valley, including antiquities found in the region, pottery and figurines. Natural and economic history, Haganah Museum.

HAIFA [EB]
Dagon Museum
Plumer Square. Visit by arrangement. Guided tour daily (except Friday) 10.30.
Founded in 1955 by Dr. R. Hecht. Archaeological museum showing handling of grain through the ages; Chalcolithic and Bronze Age-Iron Age silos from various sites.

Ethnology and Folklore Museum
Arlosoroff Street 19. Monday and Wednesday 10–1, 4–7; Sunday, Tuesday, Thursday and Friday 10–1.
Founded 1956 by the Haifa Municipality. Contains a collection of Jewish ritual objects of popular type; dresses and textiles of Oriental Jews and Palestinian Arabs; ethnological collection of objects from Asia.

Maritime Museum
Ha-Namal Street 2. Weekdays 8.30–12.30.
Founded in 1949 by the Israel Navy on the basis of the collection of E. Ben-Eli. Taken over in 1955 by Haifa Municipality. Models of ancient ships, sea maps, coins with naval symbols, archaeological finds; modern warfare, including the spoils of the Egyptian destroyer Ibrahim el Awal.

Museum of Ancient Art
Town Hall, Bialik 4. Weekdays (except Sunday) 10–1, 4–7; Saturday, holidays and holiday eves 10–1.
Founded in 1949 by the Haifa Municipality based on the collection of the late A. Rosh. Roman sculpture (portrait figures of Roman times, sarcophagi of Sidamara type), pottery and bronze figurines from Egypt, Palestine, Greece and Italy. Door of a Jewish tomb from Tamra. Glass and pottery vessels of the Hellenistic to Byzantine periods. Jewish and city coins of the Hellenistic to Roman periods. Coptic textiles and wax portraits from Egyptian burials. Finds from the excavations of Tell Abu Huwwam and Shikmona.

Museum of Japanese Art
Shderot ha-Nassi 89. Weekdays (except Friday) 10–1, 4–7; Saturday and holidays 10–2.
Founded 1960 by the Haifa Municipality based upon the collection of Felix Tikotin. Architects: M. Rubichek and W. Anker. Drawings, sketches and prints mainly of the 17th and 18th centuries, woodcuts, applied art in metal, lacquer, small sculptures, porcelain and pottery of the 18th and 19th centuries.

Museum of Modern Art
Town Hall, Bialik 4. Weekdays (except Sunday) 10–1, 4–7; Saturday, holidays and holiday eves 10–1.
Founded 1951 by Haifa Municipality. Paintings of contemporary artists from Israel and abroad, graphic arts, posters, mosaics and ceramics, sculptures.

Prehistory and Natural History Museums
Hatishbi Street 124. Monday and Thursday 8–1, 4–6; Sunday, Tuesday and Wednesday 8–1; Friday and holiday eves 8–12; Saturday and holidays 9–1.
Founded 1952 (Natural History) and 1962 (Prehistory) by Haifa Municipality. The prehistory collection resulted from the archaeological survey of Haifa and vicinity; it includes dioramas and reconstructions of prehistoric cultures, tools of the various periods, anatomical comparisons of modern and prehistoric man, reconstructions of two Neolithic houses from the Oren Valley.

HANITA [DB]
Regional Museum
Summer weekdays 9–12, 4–6; Friday and holiday eves 9–12; Saturday and holidays 9–6. Winter, daily 9–12; Saturday and holidays 9–6.
Founded in 1952 by members of the kibbutz. Housed in Arab-style house built on ruins of Byzantine church. Archaeological collection illustrating local history: prehistoric flints and reconstructed vessels from the Chalcolithic period; pottery, bronze objects and figurines from Middle and Late Bronze Age; mosaics from Byzantine church and model of church. Collection illustrating the history of the settlement since 1938; natural history collection.

HAZOREA
Wilfrid Israel House for Oriental Art and Studies
Saturday and holidays 10–12.30, 5–6.30; Tuesday 8–9.
Founded by Hazorea kibbutz in memory of Wilfrid Israel (died 1943 on a mission to Europe) and based on his collection. Architect: A. Mansfeld. Collection of ancient Mediterranean art; Egyptian figurines and reliefs; Greek Tanagra figurines; Roman figurines; Coptic textiles. Ancient Persian pottery; Luristan bronzes. Far East and South Asian collection: India, Cambodia, Thailand, China, Japan; includes Khmer head of Buddha and Chinese painted scrolls. Archaeological finds from the region, especially of the Chalcolithic and Middle Bronze periods.

HEBRON [HB]
Municipal Museum
On road from Jerusalem.
Antiquities and illustrative material from the site.

JERUSALEM [GC]
Flagellatio Monastery of the Studium Biblicum Franciscanum
Via Dolorosa, Old City. Open by arrangement.
Antiquities from the Franciscan excavations at Bethany, Dominus flevit etc.

Herbert E. Clarke Collection of Near Eastern Antiquities
Y.M.C.A., 26 David Street. Monday to Saturday 10–1.
Founded in 1933 based on the collection of H. E. Clarke, American consul in Jerusalem in Turkish times. Prehistoric flints and tools, Bronze Age pottery and alabaster vessels, scarabs; Israelite pottery, lamps, figurines; Roman bronzes and glass, beads and Greek vases.

Herzl Museum
Mount Herzl. Sunday, Monday, Tuesday 8–1, 3–5; Friday, Saturday and holidays 8–1.
Founded in 1960 by the Zionist Organization on the centenary of the birth of Dr Theodore Herzl, the founder of the organization, who conceived the idea of a Jewish State. Tomb of Herzl (his remains were brought over from Vienna in 1949 after the foundation of the State of Israel), Herzl's working room, documents and library.

Isaac Wolfson Museum
Hekhal Shelomoh (Chief Rabbinate), King George Avenue 28. Weekdays 10–1, Friday and holiday eves 10–12.
Founded in 1958 by the Hekhal Shelomoh. Collection of Jewish ritual amulets, textiles, seals of Chief Rabbis of the Turkish period, ancient illustrations of Jewish holy sites.

Israel Museum
Ruppin Street. Daily (except Tuesday) 10–6; Tuesday 4–10; Friday and Saturday 10–2.
Founded 1965 by the amalgamation of the Bezalel Art Museum, the collection of the Department of Antiquities, and the Shrine of the Book. The main building was planned by A. Mansfeld, A. Noy and D. Gad, the Shrine of the Book by F. Wiesler and A. Bartos, the Billy Rose Sculpture Garden by Isamu Noguchi.

Bezalel National Art Museum was founded in 1906 by Boris Schatz together with the Bezalel Art School. From 1932 to 1957 it was developed by M. Narkiss into one of the largest collections of Jewish art, past and present. A component of the Israel Museum since 1965.
The first exhibition on entering the halls of the museum is of Jewish ritual objects, arranged by subject: the Torah scroll and its ornaments, the Sabbath, New Year, the Day of Atonement, tabernacles (includes a painted sukkah from Germany of the 19th century), Hannukah lamp exhibit, Purim, Pessah and the family feasts. With this are exhibited the wooden doors of the Fustat syagogue of Maimonides. The next exhibition is of illuminated Hebrew manuscripts, including Rothschild MS. 24 from Italy of the Renaissance period and the famous "birds' head" Haggadah—a German manuscript of the 14th century. Next are exhibited examples of Jewish costumes from Yemen, Bokhara, Kurdistan, Morocco, Algeria, Persia. Adjoining the costume collection is the complete synagogue of Vittorio Veneto in Italy (18th century), which was brought over and reconstructed in the museum, and another synagogue from Horb (Germany) also of the 18th century, with a painted roof. A section is devoted to ancient Persian art, including pottery and Luristan bronzes, figurines and gold and silver vessels from the Achaemenid and Sassanian period; Islamic pottery and a blue-glazed tile mihrab (praying niche) from Isfahan of the 17th century.
The section on contemporary art shows a selection of European artists: Courbet, Renoir, Sisley, Cézanne, Van Gogh, Gauguin, Braque, Picasso, Chagall, Soutine, Pascin, Schiele, Kokoschka, Bacon, Ben Nicholson, Appel; of American artists: Gorky, de Kooning and Morris Louis; and of Israeli artists: Ardon, Aroch, Arikha, Zaritzky. An 18th-century room of the banker Samuel Bernard by the architect Boffrand, which had been the working room of Baron Edmond de Rothschild, was reconstructed in the museum.
The Billy Rose Sculpture Garden. The open air section has sculpture by Rodin (*Adam, Balzac*), Calder, Bourdelle, Maillol, Moore, Lipchitz, Picasso (*Profile de Femme*), Vasarély (*Screen*), Tinguely etc. In the Lipchitz Pavilion is an exceptional collection of 130 works by the artist.
The Samuel Bronfman Biblical and Archaeological Museum is based on the collection of the Department of Antiquities and Museums of the Government of Israel, which was begun in 1948; in addition there are objects from the collection of the Institute of Archaeology of the Hebrew University and from private collections. The museum was opened as part of the Israel Museum in 1965; in 1971 it was enlarged by a gallery of Byzantine to Crusader art, a coin exhibition and an exhibition of objects from the neighbouring countries. The exhibition is arranged in periods and includes Chalcolithic ivories and ossuaries, metal objects from the "Cave of the Treasure" in the Hever Valley, objects from the temples of Hazor and Nahariya of the Middle Bronze

Age, Philistine ware, a reconstructed fortress gate from Israelite Hazor, two altars from the Arad sanctuary, proto-Aeolic capitals and the "balustrade" from Ramat Rahel, inscriptions in Old Hebrew script, including the Mezad Hashavyahu letter, Arad ostraca, seals and the Amaziah cave inscription, objects from Nabatean Avdat, from Masada, the furniture and pottery from a Herodian house in the old city of Jerusalem, the sarcophagus from the Tomb of the Nazirite Jerusalem, a selection of ossuaries, the famous inscription from Caesarea mentioning Pontius Pilate, sculpture from Caesarea, Beth Shean and other sites (the Artemis of Ephesus, the Erex griffon, synagogue mosaic from Yafia and Beth Shean, Jewish lead coffins, seals, encolpia and other objects, Late Roman mosaics and sculptures, Islamic pottery and jewelry, Crusader sculpture.

Shrine of the Book (also open on Tuesday 10-10) contains collection of the Dead Sea scrolls originally found in 1947: two Isaiah scrolls, the Book of the Covenant, the Thanksgiving scroll, the Book of the War of the Sons of Light with the Sons of Darkness, the Habakkuk commentary, the Genesis apocryphon. In addition are exhibited writings found in the Nahal Hever "Cave of the Letters" with official and private documents from the time of the Bar Kokhba war: fifteen letters from Bar Kokhba's headquarters in Hebrew, Aramaic and Greek, and 35 private documents, mostly legal, from the archives of a woman called Babatha, who found refuge in the same cave. There are also a few documents found in the excavations of Masada. A few of the objects found in the cave of Nahal Hever are exhibited in the corridor leading to the domed room in which the scrolls are exhibited.

The Youth Wing contains exhibitions of archaeology, ethnology and contemporary artists.

Library of the Armenian Patriarchate
St James, Old City. Visit by arrangement.
Armenian illuminated manuscripts.

Library of the Greek Orthodox Patriarchate
Christian Street, Old City. Visit by arrangement.
Illuminated manuscripts.

Model of Jerusalem of the Second Temple
Holyland Hotel. Summer 8–5; winter 8–4.
1:50 scale model (40 x 25 m.) of Jerusalem in AD 66, built as open air model under the direction of M.

Avi-Yonah, after drawing by Eva Avi-Yonah. Completed in 1969.

Museum of Islamic Antiquities
Haram esh-Sharif, Bab el Maghrebin. Daily (except Friday) 8–11, 1–5.
Founded by the Moslem Supreme Council. Koran manuscripts, objects found in the Temple area, Islamic art.

Museum of Musical Instruments
Rubin Music Academy, Smolenskin 7. Daily 10–1.
Founded in 1963 by Music Academy. Musical instruments of various periods and peoples, arranged by subject: idiophonic, membrophonic, aerophonic and cordophonic.

Rockefeller Museum
Jericho Road. Daily 10–6; Friday and Saturday 10–2.
The building was a gift of John D. Rockefeller and was opened by the Department of Antiquities of the Mandatory Government in 1938. It housed the collection of finds made in archaeological excavations 1920-48. Now administered by the Israel Museum. The South Octagon contains the statue of Rameses III and the Lion Relief, as well as other objects from Beth Shean. The South Gallery contains a chronological collection of finds from the prehistoric and Bronze Age periods. It includes skulls and skeletons from the Carmel caves and Neolithic Jericho, Mesolithic sculpture, the Hederah ossuary, finds from the Early Bronze sanctuary at Ai, the earliest examples of alphabetic writing from Shechem, the Jericho head vase, Late Bronze finds from Beth Shean and Lachish, jewelry from Beth Aglayim. The central part of the museum contains Islamic remains (carved beams from the el-Aqsa mosque, stucco sculpture from Khirbet Mefjer) and Crusader remains, such as lintels from the Holy Sepulchre. Two side rooms are devoted to the exhibition of coins and jewelry. The North Gallery continues the chronological arrangement of exhibits from the Iron Age to the Arab period; it includes Megiddo ivories, the anthropoid coffins from Beth Shean, the incense stands from the same site, the Achziv statuettes, the Athlith Aphrodite, fragment of an inscription from the Second Temple, glass and pottery of the Roman periods, Byzantine bronze and glassware, Arabic manuscripts from Khirbet el Mird in the Judaean desert, a reconstructed Hyksos tomb, and some Roman sculptures. In the North Octagon Jewish symbols (seven branched candlesticks) from various sites are exhibited. In the court of the museum are the Caesarea sarcophagi and other large sculptures.

Schocken Library
Balfour Street 6. Sunday to Wednesday 9–1, 4–8; Thursday 9–1.
Based on the collection of Zalman Schocken and transferred in 1935 to Jerusalem. Hebrew manuscripts including Nuremberg Mahzor of 1331, Bible of the 13th century, Nuremberg Haggadas (14th and 15th centuries), incunabula, graphic art.

Yad va-Shem Memorial of the Victims of the Holocaust
Har ha-Zikaron. Daily 9–5; Friday and holiday eves 9–2.
Founded 1957; opened 1960. Memorial Hall, with gates by D. Palombo, exhibition of documents and illustrations.

LOHAMEY HA-GETABT [DB]

Ghetto Fighters Memorial Museum
Daily 9–4; Friday and holiday eves 9–2; Saturday and holidays 10–5.
Founded 1951; building by S. Bickels opened 1959. Documents, photographs and models of the Holocaust, the Ghetto revolts and the resistance movement.

MAAGAN MICHAEL [EB]

Underwater Archaeology Museum
Open by arrangement.
Founded in 1959 by the kibbutz. Contains pottery (especially wine jars) pulled out of the sea by fishermen, Myceanean pottery, Phoenician wares and Greek armour.

MAAYAN BARUKH [DC]

Regional Prehistoric Museum of the Huleh Valley
Weekdays 9–12, Saturday and holidays by arrangement.
Founded in 1955 by members of the kibbutz. Palaeolithic hand-axes, Neolithic and Chalcolithic microliths, Early Bronze pottery, Roman lamps and glass, stone hand-mills and oil presses.

NAZARETH [EC]

Museum of the Terra Sancta Convent
Monday to Saturday 7–6; Sunday and Catholic holidays 7–12.
Founded by the Franciscan Fathers in 1922. Finds from the Crusader Church of the Annunciation, including capitals with scenes from the life of Jesus. French sculpture of the 12th century. Other finds made in Nazareth and vicinity.

NIR DAVID [EC]

Museum of Mediterranean Archaeology
Monday, Tuesday, Saturday and holidays 10–3.

Founded in 1963, based on the collection of Dan Lifshitz. Architects: S. Powsner, R. Abraham and E. Rogen. Includes a collection of small objects from Greece, Rome, Etruria and South Italy from the archaic period to the second century AD. Archaic painted pottery and figurines from classical Athens, moulds for figurines from Tarentum of the archaic to Hellenistic periods, Hellenistic stone reliefs from Tarentum, figurines from Tanagra and Attica, female head from Phoenicia, pottery. Roman glass and terra sigillata, Etruscan pottery of the Villanova type, gold jewelry and bronze objects from Etruria, Etruscan and South Italian painted pottery, medieval Persian ceramics. Exhibition of finds from excavations on the site, Bronze and Iron Ages.

SAFED [DC]

Glicenstein Museum of Art
Weekdays 9–12, 3–6; Friday, Saturday and holidays 9–12.
Founded in 1953 by the Glicenstein family and Safed Municipality, in former residence of Turkish kaimakan. Sculptures of H. Glicenstein; collection of paintings of European artists.

Museum of the Printing Arts
Artists' Quarter. Weekdays 10–1, 3–5; Friday 10–1; Saturday 3–6.
Founded in 1953 in Jerusalem, transferred to Safed in 1961, as the town where Hebrew printing was begun in the Ottoman empire in 1577. Models of presses, incunabula of the 15th century, rare books and prints.

SEDOT YAM [EB]

Caesarea Museum
Daily 9–12.
Founded in 1952 by members of the kibbutz. Contains finds from Caesarea and vicinity of the Hellenistic, Roman, Byzantine, Arab, Crusader and Mameluke periods, arranged by subject: lamps, glass, pottery, figurines, jewelry, gems, seals, etc. Coins found at Caesarea. Roman-Byzantine sculpture, including torso of imperial statue of second century; inscriptions, including Jewish tombstones, the epitaph of a Roman officer who served in the Tenth and Sixth legions; architectural fragments: capitals and column fragments; pottery found in the sea.

SHAAR HA-GOLAM [EC]

Museum of Prehistory
Daily 9–11, 4–6.
Founded in 1950 by the members of the regional prehistory circle.

Collection of objects illustrating the Neolithic Yarmukian culture found in the vicinity. The objects are exhibited so as to illustrate the way of life and work of the first agricultural farmers in the Holy Land: tools, beginnings of pottery craft, fertility cults and figurines, manufacture of flints.

TEL AVIV [FB]

Haaretz Museum
Ramat Aviv. Sunday and Wednesday 10–8; Monday, Tuesday, Thursday and holidays 10–5; Friday, Saturday and holiday eves 10–1.

Sections:

Glass Museum was founded in 1950 by the Municipality, based on the collection of Dr W. Moses. Architects: Witkower and Baumann. Illustrates the manufacture of glass in the various periods, from sand-core vessels, to moulded and blown glass. Glass from the Late Bronze and Israelite periods, drawn on a sand core; Hellenistic moulded glass; Early Roman period blown glass, including blue glass vase signed Ennion; glass decorated with reliefs; Byzantine Jewish glass; Christian glasses, *fondi d'oro.* Blown glass in various shapes and ornaments. Arab period: mosque lamp of the 13th century from Cairo. Modern glass from the 17th century onwards.

Ceramics Museum is based on the Moses collection, opened in 1966. Beginning of pottery in Palestine; technical processes from the primitive hand-made pottery to wheel-made wares; pottery and its use in daily life; pottery in the service of archaeology; pottery in art and religion.

Kadman Numismatic Museum was founded in 1962 from the Moses and Kadman collections. Architects: Witkower and Baumann. The collection includes examples of means of payment before the invention of coinage; a model of an ancient mint; Greek coins; coins of Palestine, including Jewish coins and coins of Aelia Capitolina; Near Eastern coins; coins of the various periods from the Roman to the Mandatory; coins of the State of Israel; paper money; coins as ornament; weights and scales of various periods.

Museum of Ethnography and Folklore was founded in 1963, based on the Gniza collection of Jewish popular art and the collection of the National Costume Society. Jewish ritual objects arranged by holidays, candlesticks, Jewish art, marriage deeds,

the Kai-Feng-Fu (China) Jewish community, Jewish costumes, jewelry and amulets. Architects: Witkower and Baumann.

Museum of Science and Technology was founded by P. Fiatli and A. Moskowitch and opened in 1964. Illustrates by models, graphs, diagrams, and instruments, especially the following subjects: aeronautics and astronautics, mathematics and the Foucauld pendulum, energy and communications.

Tel Qasile, the archaeological site of the Late Bronze to Iron Age is conserved within the Haaretz Museum.

Historical Museum of Tel Aviv
Bialik Street 26. Sunday and Wednesday 9–2, 5–7; Monday, Tuesday, Thurday and Friday and holiday eves 9–2; Saturday 10–1.
Founded in 1956 in the Shenkar House. Documents, maps and illustrations, models and photographs of the development of Tel Aviv since its foundation in 1909.

Man and His Works (Adam ve-Amalo)
Beeri Street 14. Sunday and Wednesday 11–1, 6–8; Monday, Tuesday, Thursday 11–1; holiday eves 11–1.
Founded in 1943 by the Folklore Group and the Avshalom Institute of the General Federation of Labour. Illustrates the working tools and processes of hunters and farmers, transport and communication, energetics, light, writing, weights and measures; the materials used: organic and inorganic (metallic and non-metallic); open air museum of agricultural installations.

Museum of the Alphabet
Bialik Street 26. Sunday and Wednesday 9–2, 5–7; Monday, Tuesday, Thursday and Friday and holiday eves 9–12; Saturday 10–1.
Founded in 1965 by D. Diringer. Illustrates the development of writing, from pre-literate ways of communicating to the alphabet (with special stress on the development of the Hebrew alphabet), with samples of the most important inscriptions demonstrating this development.

Museum of Antiquities of Tel Aviv-Jaffa
Mifratz Shelomo Street 10. Sunday and Wednesday 10–8; Monday, Tuesday and Thursday 10–5; Friday, Saturday, holidays and holiday eves 10–1.
Founded in 1951 in 19th-century Turkish house. Finds from the Tel Aviv-Jaffa excavations in chronological order: Neolithic and Chalcolithic

finds, including fertility figurines and ossuaries; Bronze Age including Hyksos weapons; part of the gate of Jaffa with the name of Pharaoh Rameses II; Israelite finds from Tel Qasile; objects of the Hasmonaean period, including a small glass amphora and other glass vessels and lamps; pottery and weights of the Roman period.

Tel Aviv Museum
King Saul Boulevard. Daily 10–1, 4–7; Friday and Saturday 10–1.
Founded 1932 by M. Dizengoff, the first mayor of Tel Aviv. In the Helena Rubinstein Pavilion, opened in 1958, shows by Israeli and foreign artists are held. The new building, by architects Isaac Yashar and Dan Eytan, was opened in 1971. It houses the museum's collections and most of the major temporary shows. Representative collection of Israeli artists since the beginning of the century. Paintings by French Impressionists. Post-Impressionist artists such as James Ensor, Utrillo, Vlaminck are represented by several works. Contemporary painters such as Max Ernst, Jackson Pollock, and artists of the Paris School. Jewish

artists from the Diaspora. The sculpture collection includes several painted reliefs by Archipenko and monumental works by Lipchitz and Moore. The activity of the museum consists mainly in temporary exhibitions, lectures, concerts and film evenings.

Zahal (Israel Defence Forces) Museum
Rothschild Boulevard 23. Weekdays 10–5; Friday, Saturday and holidays 10–1.
Opened in 1961 in the house of the late Haganah commander E. Golomb. Illustrates the history of the Haganah and the Israel army from 1921 to 1949.

TIBERIAS [EC]
Municipal Museum
On the coast. Summer weekdays 8–12, 4–7; Friday and Saturday 8–12. Winter weekdays 8–12, 5–8; Friday and Saturday 8–12.
Founded in 1952 by the late Tirzah Ravani. Collection of local antiquities, including doors and other stone reliefs of the Roman and Byzantine periods, inscription, a lion from Chorazin, menoroth from Tiberias, coins, Hittite reliefs.

Cities and Archaeological Sites

Abu Ghosh [GB]
Arab village 12 km. west of Jerusalem at foot of biblical site of Kiryat Yearim or Baalah (*Joshua 15:9, 60: 18:14;* etc.). The village is called after a famous bandit chief of the early 19th century who levied tolls on pilgrims and travellers going up to Jerusalem; its proper name is Qiryat el Inab. The local spring has attracted settlers from prehistoric periods onwards. A post of the Tenth Legion and later Arab and Mameluke khans were situated here. From 1141 to 1187 it was held by the Hospitallers (Order of St John) who built a Romanesque church there over a crypt with the spring (14.3 x x 7.5 m.). The church has walls 4 m. thick, a triple apse and cross vaults resting on six pillars. It was restored by Mauss in the 19th century.

Acre (Accho, Ptolemais, St Jean d'Acre) [DB]
Phoenician harbour city at the north

end of the Haifa Bay. The Bronze Age settlement was at Tell el Fukhkhar (Napoleon's Hill) east of the city. Owing to its strong position on the coast with two harbours, Accho was not conquered by the Israelites under Joshua (*Judges 1:31*) but remained a Phoenician city. In Persian times the town was in its present site and was regarded as a royal fortress, the main Persian base against Egypt. Alexander established a royal mint there. Under Ptolemy II Philadelphus Acre was first called Ptolemais, a name kept till the Arab invasion. It resisted the Hasmonaeans successfully, and served as a base for both Herod and Vespasian in their campaigns against Judaea. Acre became a Roman colony under Claudius. It served from the 2nd century onward as the main harbour of Galilee, and included a considerable Jewish population; on occasion it was visited by the Jewish patriarchs, one of whom bathed there at the Baths of Aphrodite. Ptolemais was visited by Paul the Apostle (*Acts 12:7*) and had one of the earliest Christian communities in Palestine. It was captured by the Arabs and resumed its Semitic name (Akka). In the 10th century Ahmad ibn Tulun enlarged the harbour. In 1104 it was taken by the Crusaders, lost in 1187 but regained from Saladin in a famous siege, by Richard Coeur de Lion and Philippe Auguste of France, in 1191. From that date to 1291 it was the capital of the second Crusader kingdom. Crusader Acre was the headquarters of the Hospitallers and Templars of the Italian colonies (from Venice, Genoa, Pisa, etc.) and had the first Franciscan convent in the Holy Land (1219). It fell to the Mamelukes in 1291 and was completely destroyed. In the 16th century it was rebuilt by the Druze emir Fakhr-el-din. In the 18th century it became the headquarters of the Bedouin sheikh Dhahr-el-Omar, who set up its walls and ruled Galilee from there. He was replaced by the Bosnian adventurer Ahmed Pasha, nicknamed Jazzar ("the Butcher"). Jazzar withstood Napoleon in the siege of 1799. He afterwards strengthened the fortifications of Acre; the walls existing now are his work; with later additions by the Egyptian Ibrahim Pasha. Acre remained the headquarters of northern Palestine under Jazzar's successors till its occupation by the Egyptians in 1832. A bombardment by an Anglo-Austrian fleet restored Turkish rule in 1840. It declined with the rise of Haifa. It was taken by the Israeli Army on 18 May 1948; a new town has been added to the Old City since.

The Citadel of Acre (now a mental hospital) can be visited in some parts. The main remains in the city are the mosque of Jazzar with his tomb (1804), a refectory of the Order of St John under the citadel with a vault resting on three huge pillars, the Pasha's bath (now the municipal museum) and a Turkish market (1810). The walls of Acre, consisting of a double line with bastions, a fosse and counterscarps, have been restored as a park.

Ashdod [GA]

Canaanite city founded in the 16th century BC, it became, in the 12th century BC, one of the cities of the Philistine pentapolis (*Joshua 11:22*). The Ark of the Law, captured by the Philistines, was brought to the Temple of Dagon at Ashdod with disastrous consequences (*1 Samuel 5*). The walls of Ashdod were breached by Uzziah of Judah (2 *Chronicles 26:6*). In 711 BC Ashdod was captured by the Assyrians and became the headquarters of a province, which it remained till Persian times (*Nehemiah 13:23-24*). It was conquered by the Hasmonaeans and freed by the Romans; in the Byzantine period a new town rose by the sea (*Azotus Paralius*). The excavations of the site have been carried on since 1962. Twenty different levels have been uncovered, including the remains of a Philistine gate, an acropolis, a lower craftsman's quarters round a sanctuary.

6 km. north of the ancient site the modern city of Ashdod has been built, beginning in 1957. It has the second deep-water harbour of Israel, industrial installations and a modern civic centre, in the middle of which is a sculpture by Yigael Tumarkin.

Ashkelon (ancient **Ascalon**) [GA]

The Ashkelon National Park (including the ruins) is maintained by the Parks Authority. April to September 8–5, October to March 8–4.

Canaanite city, mentioned in Egyptian texts of the 19th century BC, it was mostly dominated by Egypt (with occasional revolts as in the time of Rameses II, 1280 BC) and Merneptah. In the 12th century BC it became one of the principal Philistine cities (*Joshua 13:3*). Later it came under Assyrian suzerainty, against which it revolted under Sargon II, Sennacherib and Assurbanipal. It contained a famous temple of Aphrodite Urania, mentioned by Herodotus (I, 105). In Persian times Ascalon was a Tyrian town; it was thoroughly Hellenized under the Ptolemies. Ascalon kept its independence under the Hasmonaeans, and remained an "allied city" under Rome. Herod, who was born there, adorned the city. In Late Roman times Ascalon had a school of philosophy and was one of the centres of paganism. It was taken by the Arabs and fortified by the Fatimids. The Crusaders took it in 1153, after it had served as a Muslim base, and held it till 1187, and again from 1191 to 1247. It was ruined by Baybars in 1270.

The ruins of Ascalon form a semi-circular area bounding on the Mediterranean; on the seashore the accumulated strata can be observed together with column shafts used to strengthen the walls. The whole area is enclosed by Byzantine walls, repaired in the Crusader period; they are built of a combination of brick and stone. The excavated area includes a city hall (*bouleuterion*) of semi-circular shape with an adjoining portico. Originally founded by Herod, it was reconstructed in the time of the Severan dynasty (2nd-3rd centuries AD). The remains include reliefs of the goddess of Victory (Nike) holding a palm branch and standing on the celestial globe, which is supported by a crouching Atlas. Another fragment of sculpture has the relief of Isis and Harpocrates, indicating the strong Egyptian influence in Ascalon, even in Roman times. Isis is shown with her fringed cloak and knot in front, with the high Pharaonic crown.

A modern summer resort—Ashkelon-Afridar—has been built north of the ancient ruins since 1953, mainly by settlers from South Africa. In the civic centre there is a small museum of antiquities. In the courtyard, a relief in red brick by Shalom Sebba.

Athlith

Phoenician port and Crusader castle 20 km. south of Haifa, on the coast. The Phoenician remains date from the Persian period and represent a settlement of Greek mercenaries who married native women. The Crusader fortress was built by pilgrims (hence its name, Château des Pèlerins) of the Fifth Crusade. It was held by the Templars till they evacuated it in 1291. A Crusader city with a separate wall and a corner fort adjoined the castle which is built on a promontory and protected by a fosse running from sea to sea. The castle has a double wall, with the high towers of the second line dominating the outer wall. Inside the great north tower was a vaulted hall. Other vaults, some of them underground, line the shore. The church of the castle had an octagonal shape, recalling the Dome of the Rock in Jerusalem, which the Crusaders regarded as the "Templum Domini".

Avdat (ancient **Eboda**) [JB]

Maintained by the National Parks Authority. April to September 8–5; October to March 8–4.

Nabatean-Byzantine town, 65 km. south of Beersheba in the Negev wilderness. Founded by the Nabateans about 300 BC, it became the burial place of King Obodas who was deified as Zeus Obodas; his successor Aretas IV (9 BC-AD 40) built a temple in his honour. Avdat was an important caravan centre on the Petra-Gaza and Elath-Gaza roads. It was abandoned in the first quarter of the 2nd century AD, resettled late in the 3rd century and became a flourishing Byzantine town until after the Arab conquest when it was gradually abandoned. The remains, excavated in 1958-60, include a Nabatean podium and staircases, tombs and agricultural remains, a Late Roman town and tombs, and Byzantine underground dwellings and two churches. The northern one (which is the earlier), of basilical type with a single apse, contains the seat of the bishop. The church has an atrium with a well; near it, on the Nabatean podium, is a baptistry lined with marble. A Nabatean gate to the acropolis has been preserved in its northern side. The southern church was dedicated to St Theodore; it has three apses and a chancel screen. Inscriptions found in the church date it to the years 541-618. Adjoining the church is a cloistered atrium which served a monastery. East of the church stands a Late Roman house. A large Byzantine fortress (61 x 41 m.) protected Avdat on the east side. A Byzantine bath of the hypocaust type stands at the foot of the city mountain. The architectural remains are of typical Byzantine desert style.

Beersheba [HB]

Biblical city, the foundation of which is attributed by tradition to Abraham (*Genesis 21:31*); the southern boundary point of the Land of Israel according to *Judges 20:1*. Biblical Beersheba is now being excavated at Tell Beersheba, an ancient mound north of the modern city; there are, however, indications that the modern site was also settled in ancient times. Beersheba, in Chalcolithic times (4000-3000 BC), was the centre of an early culture. The town continued to exist as a border city on the fringe of the Negev wilderness until the Byzantine era; it served as an administrative centre for the Palestinian limes. It was abandoned in medieval times, and revived by the Turks in 1906 under the guidance of German engineers. The kernel of the modern town with the mosque (now the museum) and war cemetery marks the Turkish town. After its occupation by the Israeli army in 1948, Beersheba was developed on a large scale as a modern city; but the Bedouins of the Negev still use it as a market and trading centre. Modern Beersheba houses the Arid Zone Research Centre, the beginnings of a university, a cultural centre, a modern hospital and some of the most interesting experiments in modern housing architecture in Israel, with special consideration for the desert conditions. At the northern entrance of the new town, buildings by the architects Yaski and

Alexandroni show the influence of Le Corbusier on Israeli architecture after 1955. The "Negev Centre" by Ram Carmi offers an interesting solution to the problems of heat und crude light with its street for pedestrians which goes through the building. An old well south of the town is still called Abraham's well.

Belvoir (Kokhav ha-Yarden, Kaukab el-Hawa) [EC]
Maintained by the National Parks Authority. April to September 8–5; October to March 8–4.
Crusader fortress overlooking the Jordan Valley, 16 km. south of the Sea of Galilee. The fortress was built by the Hospitallers after they acquired the castle from its seigneur, Ivo Velos, in 1168. It remained in the possession of the knights after the disaster at Hattin and held out for two years against Saladin till it capitulated in 1189. It was destroyed by the Muslims in 1219. The site was excavated in 1966. The castle is protected on its south, west and north sides by a deep fosse cut in the rock; on the east the ground slopes steeply to the Jordan Valley below. The outer fortifications consist of curtain walls with three towers on each side; on the east the curtain forms an angle, giving the castle a pentagonal shape, with a huge keep in the centre. The outer court, which is approached through a complicated gateway, has a well and a bath house. The inner castle is square, with towers in the corners and a tower in its west wall. It contained a kitchen, a refectory and vaults. The chapel stood in the south-west corner of the inner court.

Beth Alpha (Hefzibah) [EC]
National Monument. April to September 8–5; October to March 8–4.
Mosaic pavement and other remains of ancient synagogue, excavated in 1928 below the modern kibbutz of Hefzibah. The synagogue is dated by an inscription to the time of "King" Justin, probably the emperor Justin I (518-27). The original building consisted of an atrium, a narthex and a basilical hall, ending in an apse pointing to Jerusalem. The apse stood on a podium. The pavement is decorated with figured designs. At the entrance a lion and a bull face each other as guardians of the threshold; the dedicatory inscription in Aramaic and a Greek inscription mentioning the artists (Marinus and his son Hanina) adjoin it. The pavement of the nave is divided into three panels: nearest to the entrance is one representing the Offering of Isaac. It shows Abraham standing with a knife in his hand, with Isaac (bound) and the flaming altar to the right. A ram is seen attached to a tree on the left, above it a symbolic hand of God emerging from a cloud and the two servants with a donkey. The inscriptions are in Hebrew. The second panel shows a Zodiac, with symbols of the seasons in the corners, the images of the Zodiac in a circle around Helios (the Sun) in his chariot. The third panel, nearest the apse, shows the Ark of the Law flanked by seven-branched candlesticks and lions. The nave mosaic is surrounded by a border with rural symbols. The aisles are paved with geometric mosaic. The Beth Alpha mosaic is an outstanding example of Orientalizing Jewish village art of the Byzantine period.

Bethlehem [GB]
Town 9 km. south of Jerusalem, mentioned in the Bible in connection with the death and burial of Rachel (*Genesis 35:19*). It was the town of Boaz (*Ruth*) and hence the family town of David. Reference to its glory as the birthplace of the Messiah is found in *Micah 5:2*. Christian tradition locates the birth of Jesus at Bethlehem; according to the Church Fathers the birth took place in a cave over which stood a sanctuary of Tammuz-Adonis in pagan times. Constantine built the first basilica at Bethlehem; it ended in an octagonal structure standing over the cave. Remains of the mosaic pavements of this church are still visible inside the basilica. Justinian had the basilica rebuilt, adding a trefoil-shaped triple apse. Access to the Grotto of the Nativity is by a narrow stairway and through a Crusader portal; the bronze doors in the gates are from the time of Justinian. Within the grotto the traditional place of the Nativity is marked by a silver star of the 18th century. The Catholic church adjoining the basilica has a medieval cloister, the pilasters of which have been peeled out from later pillars.

Beth Shean (Greek Scythopolis, Arabic Beisan) [EC]
National Monument. April to September 8–5; October to March 8–4.
City in the Harod Valley close to the Jordan. Originally a Canaanite stronghold—the remains of which have been excavated on the prominent mound—it was occupied by a Philistine garrison under the Egyptians. In the time of Ptolemy II it became the Greek city of Scythopolis. Under the Byzantines it was an important centre of the textile industry and the capital of the province

of Palestina secunde. Jewish and Samaritan communities also lived here. Beth Shean declined under Arab rule, and was resettled after 1948. The visible remains include, besides the mound, the best preserved Roman theatre west of the Jordan, excavated 1961-62. The length of the *scenae frons* is 90 m.; the theatre could seat 8,000 spectators. The arrangement of the exits (*vomitoria*) is architecturally peculiar. The side entrance and the towers from which the theatre machinery was operated are still partly visible. A Roman bridge, now broken, crossed the Haron river. Beyond it a monastery was excavated by the Pennsylvania expedition which worked on the mound from 1922 to 1933. The mosaics (a village scene, a calendar with images of the months and the sun and moon in the centre) have been preserved. In one of the new quarters near the theatre the pavement of a synagogue has been unearthed, also that of a wealthy Jewish house, owned by one Kyrios Leontis, on which the Homeric myth of Odysseus and the Sirens is represented. A Samaritan synagogue was excavated in 1962 near the monastery; its mosaic pavement is now in the Israel Museum, Jerusalem. The most important finds from the Beth Shean excavations are at the Rockefeller Museum, Jerusalem, including a statue of Rameses III, a slab showing in relief two animals, the stele of the god Mekal.

Beth Shearim [EB]

National Monument. April to September 8–5; October to March 8–4.
Site of a ruined Jewish town of the Talmudic period (2nd-4th centuries AD). It was for a time the seat of the Jewish patriarch Rabbi Judah I and of his Sanhedrin. The patriarch and his family were buried there and around their tomb, in the 3rd century, a central Jewish necropolis arose, of which thirty catacombs have so far been excavated. Those buried at Beth Shearim included Jews from Phoenicia, Palmyra, Himyar in Arabia and so on. Two catacombs, No. 14 and No. 20, have been marked out by the addition of an architectural façade consisting of three arches, and an open-air praying place (orientated towards Jerusalem) above them. Catacomb No. 14 was the tomb of the patriarch and his sons, Rabbis Simeon, Gamaliel and Anina. Members of the patriarchal family, as well as other prominent rabbis, some of them martyrs for their faith, were buried in catacomb No. 20, the largest discovered, with

over 200 burials. The sarcophagi and coffins of stone which were found inside these catacombs show to what extent the representation of men and animals was allowed in Jewish art in the 3rd century; they are rather crude Orientalized imitations of classical motifs. Besides these locally made coffins, fragments of marble sarcophagi have been found, probably reused, with representations of Greek myths (one sarcophagus showing the myth of Leda and the Swan is in the Rockefeller Museum). The inscriptions at Beth Shearim are 80 per cent in Greek, the rest in Hebrew or Aramaic. In the town proper, above the catacombs, were found the remains of a synagogue, a basilica (probably used as court room and house of study), large houses and a glass factory. A huge block of crude glass, the raw material for the factories of the district, was found in one of the catacomb caves, which serves as a local museum.

Beth Yerah [EC]

Canaanite to Byzantine site at the outflow of the Jordan from the Sea of Galilee. In ancient times the town, named after the moon god, was situated east of the Jordan and was connected with the shore by a narrow neck. The Early Bronze Age fortifications secured it from that side. Excavated 1944-64 the remains include from the Early Bronze Age a Ω-shaped platform of stone, with circular foundations on top, probably a silo combined with a sanctuary. Remains of an Early Bronze wall have been found at the southern end of the ancient mound, one of the largest in Canaan. Immediately adjoining the Bronze Age remains are the remains of the Hellenistic-Roman city of Philoteria. These include a square fort (60 sq.m.) and a bath with a frigidarium provided with benches and having a pool in the centre, and a combined tepidarium and caldarium of the hypostyle type. The mosaic pavement of a 6th-century synagogue was found inside the fortress. Further north are the remains of a Byzantine church, dated to 529 and composed of atrium, narthex, a tri-apsidal basilica with an adjoining baptistry. The remains of the ancient city are within the park of the Ohalo Youth Hospice.

Caesarea [EB]

National Monument. April to September 8–5; October to March 8–4.
Formerly the Tower of Straton, a Phoenician foundation of the Persian period halfway between Haifa and Jaffa. King Herod rebuilt the city,

provided it with a harbour (the remains of which are still visible under-water) and a temple of Rome and Augustus, a theatre, a hippodrome and other buildings. It became the capital of the Roman province of Judaea, later Syria Palaestina, and remained so till the Arab conquest in 640. Vespasian made it into a Roman colony, "Colonia prima Flavia Augusta Caesariensis". In the 1st century a Christian community was established there by the Apostle Peter; here Paul was brought before the governor Felix, who sent him on to Rome. A Jewish and Samaritan community existed side by side with the pagans; the quarrel between Greeks and Jews was one of the causes of the First Revolt of 66. Hadrian stayed there during the Bar Kokhba war and a temple, the Hadraneum, was built in his honour. In Byzantine times Caesarea was the seat of an archbishopric and of a famous school of learning, illustrated by the names of Origenes and Eusebius Pamphili. It was taken by Baldwin I in 1101 and fortified in 1251 by St Louis of France. Caesarea was taken by the Mamelukes in 1265 and completely destroyed by Baybars. It has been partly excavated since 1951.

The ruins of the city have an oval shape within a Byzantine wall. On a hill outside the wall stood a church with a fine mosaic. Inside the eastern gate is the hippodrome, with huge porphyry pillars of the meta still in position. The Crusader bastioned wall and the fosse before it have been cleaned and the gateway restored. Within it are the remains of an unfinished cathedral standing on a Roman podium supported on vaults. These form part of the harbour installations. The harbour itself had to a large extent already been filled with sand in the Byzantine period. A Crusader mole, in which many porphyry and syenite columns have been re-used, juts out into the sea; on it are parts of the walls of a Crusader fortress. Outside the gateway a Byzantine open space has been cleared; it was erected together with the adjoining steps by a Byzantine city mayor, Flavius Strategius. The space was adorned by statues taken from pagan buildings; two of them, a porphyry torso of Hadrian and a composite white marble statue of Zeus are still in position. South of the Crusader town is the Roman theatre. It was first erected by Herod, but built over at least three times. The seat of the governor is still visible, as well as part of the *scenae frons*. A semi-

circular *exedra* was added to the theatre behind the scene in later times and the whole turned into a fortress in the Byzantine period. The theatre has been partly restored and is used every summer for concerts and representations during the Israel Festival. Adjoining the theatre is the kibbutz Sedoth Yam, which has a museum with objects found in Caesarea. North of the Crusader town are the remains of the "Tower of Straton" and the Jewish quarter grouped round a synagogue excavated on the seashore. At the northern end of the town two round towers of Herod's wall are visible. Beyond them stretch the two aqueducts of Caesarea: a high level one which was built by Herod and repaired by various detachments of Roman legions, as commemorated by inscriptions, and the lower level aqueduct which is later. It was used to supply water for irrigation.

Capernaum (Kefar Nahum, "Village of Nahum") [DC]
Fishermen's village on the northern shore of the Sea of Galilee. It was a favourite stopping place for Jesus, and is even called "his own city" in the Gospels (*Matthew 9:1*). Situated on the border of Galilee it had a customs house, from which the apostle Matthew was called; Peter and Andrew and several other apostles were fishermen there. The Roman garrison was commanded by a centurion, who built a synagogue and whose servant was healed by Jesus. In later ages Capernaum was known as a centre of Judaeo-Christians. Excavations on the site, which is the property of the Franciscan Custodia di Terra Santa, were begun in 1905, continued in 1921 and again since 1968. The principal remains consist of a synagogue, 3rd century—according to the latest excavators possibly 4th—and hence not the one in which Jesus preached. It is almost square (20 x 18 m.) with a façade and three portals turned to Jerusalem; the synagogue was entered from a platform in front of it with steps. Inside the building were three rows of columns, two lengthwise and one across; a small room adjoined on the northwest. On the east was a colonnaded courtyard. The north wall and colonnade have been restored. The architectural remains include a richly decorated frieze (probably once in the women's gallery above) with Jewish and magical symbols, plant and animal ornament in relief. One relief represents the Ark of the Covenant in the desert as a small temple on wheels. South of the synagogue was an

octagonal baptistry of Byzantine date paved with mosaics. The excavators have unearthed below it remains of fishermen's houses of Roman date, one of which they regard as having been the home of St Peter, later transformed into a Christian place of worship.

Chorazim [DC]
Galilean village north of Capernaum, off the Tiberias-Safed road. It is mentioned in the Gospels (*Matthew 11:21; Luke 10:13*) and in Talmudic literature. Excavations in 1905, 1926 and 1962-63 have revealed the remains of a synagogue and a village adjoining it. The synagogue is an elongated structure (23 x 17 m.) orientated southwards. Three rows of columns divide the interior, two lengthwise and one along the northern side. A terrace approached by steps stood in front of the building. The synagogue was built of hard basalt stone, which was richly carved. Remains of a "cathedra of Moses" (now in the Israel Museum) and of an ornate frieze have been found. The frieze included images of centaurs, vintage scenes and a head of a Medusa; in general the ornament of this synagogue went further in the direction of pagan art than all the others. It even included a three-dimensional figure of a lion which probably flanked the Ark of the Law (the other lion is missing).

Engeddi [HC]
Kibbutz in an oasis on the western shore of the Dead Sea. Engeddi was first mentioned in the Bible in connection with David's flight from Saul (*1 Samuel 24:1*); the vineyards of Engeddi appear in the Song of Solomon (*1:14*). It was settled in the period of the Second Temple and was an important centre of the balsam industry. During the Bar Kokhba revolt it was a command post and supply centre of the rebels, as is attested by the documents found in the Hever Valley caves. It is mentioned by Pliny as one of the centres of the Essene movement; it continued to exist as a Jewish village in Byzantine times. The remains include a Chalcolithic temple of elongated shape (20 m. long) with a sacred enclosure in front of it. The settlement of the Israelite and Persian periods is to be found on the mound called Tell Goren, excavated 1961-65. The finds of Israelite houses are evidence for the balsam factories on the spot. In the Hasmonaean period a tower was built on the mound. A Roman bath and the remains of a synagogue were found in the plain at the foot of the mound. Engeddi has a nature reserve, centred on the rich spring in the David Valley.

Eshthemoa (es-Samu') [HB]
Arab village south of Hebron. Remains of a synagogue have been excavated in the village; its west wall is still standing for a height of 9 m. The synagogue was paved with mosaics; it was a broad-house, entered through a foreroom in the east, with a niche for prayer in the northern wall. Eshthemoa is mentioned in the Bible among the cities of Judah (*Joshua 15:50; 21:14; etc.*) as a city of the Levites. It remained a Jewish village in Byzantine times, as part of the area known as 'Daromas' (the South).

Gaza [HA]
Arab city situated near the southern coast of Israel. Gaza served as an Egyptian stronghold from early times; from the 12th century BC it was one of the cities of the Philistines; Samson perished there by bringing down the house of Dagon with all the lords of the Philistines (*Judges 16*). Gaza flourished in the Hellenistic period as the terminal of the Nabatean trade route from Elath and from Petra. It was taken by Alexander Jannaeus but freed by Pompey, and continued as an important centre of paganism throughout the Roman period, and well into the 5th century. Its people worshipped Marnas, a Cretan god. In the Muslim period Gaza was for a time the capital of the whole of southern Palestine; an important Jewish and Samaritan community existed there. Gaza was a Turkish stronghold in the first world war. It declined somewhat in the times of the Mandate, but rose to new importance when it was occupied by the Egyptians in 1948 and became the capital of the 'Gaza strip', full of refugee camps. It was taken by Israeli forces in 1956-57 and again in 1967. The city is modern to a large extent; the main building is the Great Mosque, a Crusader church of the 13th century with re-used columns from a synagogue. A synagogue was excavated in 1968 on the coast.

Gerizim, Mount [FC]
Mountain, 881 m. above sea level, sacred to the Samaritans, who established their temple there after they separated from the Judaistic creed in Persian times. In the Hellenistic period a temple of Zeus Xenios was erected on the mountain and was rebuilt in the Roman period. Remains of this temple have been excavated recently. It was connected with the city of Neapolis (Nablus)

below it by a staircase, represented on coins, of which traces have also been found. The Samaritan place of sacrifice on Passover is on a second peak. It was taken over by the Byzantines, who erected an octagonal church there in 484; it was enclosed within a fortified zone by the emperor Justinian after 529.

Gibeon
Canaanite and Israelite city, 12 km. northeast of Jerusalem, now the Arab village of el Jib. Gibeon was the head city of the Hivvite confederation which made an alliance with Joshua (*Joshua 9*). Its inhabitants remained an important cultic centre till the days of Josiah. The pool of Gibeon served as a place of encounter between the forces of David and those of the House of Saul (*2 Samuel 2:12-17*). Gibeon was resettled after the First Return to Zion and is still mentioned in connection with the Roman assault on Jerusalem in AD 70. The site was excavated 1957-62. An extensive water system was discovered, including a pool cut in the rock (diameter 11.8 m., depth 10.8 m.) with a circular staircase. Near it a stepped tunnel descended for 24 m. to a spring situated outside the city wall; 3,000 tons of stone were moved in cutting these water works. Among the finds at Gibeon was also an extensive winery, with vats holding 95,000 litres of wine. Many jar handles with names of the owners of the vineyards were found in this area.

Haifa [EB]
Principal city and harbour of northern Israel. Haifa is mentioned in Byzantine and Talmudic sources of the 4th century. A Muslim town when attacked by the Crusaders in 1100, it was destroyed by Baybars. The settlement revived in the 18th century, and surpassed its rival Acre at the northern end of the bay in the 20th century. The port was inaugurated in 1931. In 1948 Haifa was taken over by the Israeli army. It has since developed over Mount Carmel and into the industrial area in Haifa Bay. Among its buildings are the Dagon silo near the harbour, the Municipal Museum of Modern and Ancient Art, a Naval Museum, and the shrine of the Bahai sect within a Persian garden, whose golden domed building is a prominent landmark.
The Haifa Technion is the principal technical institute of Israel: it has been rehoused on Mount Carmel. Outstanding is the Mechanical Engineering faculty building by Zvi Hecker and Alfred Neumann. In the Carmel Centre the Theatre of Beth Rothschild is being constructed by Alfred Mansfield. Also under construction is the Haifa University, on the Haifa-Usfyia road, based on plans by the Brazilian architect Oscar Niemeyer.

Hammath Tiberias [EC]
National Monument. April to September 8–5; October to March 8–4.
City built south of Tiberias, on the shore of the Sea of Galilee, around hot springs which are still being exploited for their medicinal values. The site, which is mentioned in the Bible (*Joshua 19:35*), became an important Jewish town in the Talmudic period. Remains of two synagogues were found there, one in 1921 and the other in 1961-63. The latter, which is the only one visible, showed three superimposed levels of buildings of the 2nd, 4th and 6th centuries. The most interesting is the synagogue of the 4th century. It is a roughly square building (13 x 15 m.) divided by three rows of columns into a basilical part of nave and two aisles, with an annex on the east. The southern part of the structure was separated from the rest by a dividing wall. The central part of this southern structure served as repository of the Thorah scrolls; a low podium in front of it was the place of prayer. The mosaic pavements provide the main interest in this synagogue, especially that of the nave which is divided into three parts. The one nearest to the entrance shows the images of two lions, with dedicatory inscriptions in Greek between them. The middle part, some of which has been ruined by a later wall, shows the image of a Zodiac with Helios-Apollo as a charioteer in the centre. The symbols of the Zodiac show some strongly classical features, for instance the Virgin is identical with the image of Kore-Persephone, Balance with Minos, Aquarius is a naked boy, and so on. In the corners are the four Seasons, each with its appropriate sign. The Hammath mosaic is the finest and most 'permissive' of the extant synagogue mosaics.

Hazor [DC]
National Monument. April to September 8–5; October to March 8–4.
Canaanite and Israelite city, first mentioned in the Egyptian execration texts of 1900 BC, late in the Mari texts of the 18th century, the el-Amarna texts of the 14th century, and the 13th-century papyrus Anastasi I. In the Bible it is called 'the head of all these kingdoms' of northern Canaan (*Joshua 11:10*); it was

taken and burnt by the Israelites. Resettled under Solomon, it became an important fortress of Ahab, till taken and destroyed by Tiglath Pileser III of Assyria in 732 BC. Excavated in 1955-58 and in 1968-69. The ancient mound consists of an acropolis settled in Canaanite and Israelite times, and a lower city, which was only Canaanite. In the upper city there is a Solomonic casemate wall and gate, a fortress, an administrative pillared building and a deep water tunnel, all the work of Ahab. The lower city has a Canaanite gate and glacis, and several temples, one of which is subdivided into three parts (porch, sanctuary and holy of holies) parallelling Solomon's later Temple.

Hebron [HB]

Ancient Canaanite city, founded 'seven years before Zoan in Egypt', which was founded in 1720 BC (*Numbers 13:22*). Abraham bought the cave of Machpelah there as a burial site for himself and his family (*Genesis 23*). After Joshua's conquest the city was the capital of the tribe of Judah; there David reigned for seven years before becoming king over all Israel (*2 Samuel 5:5*). At present the main city of southern Jordan, inhabited by Arabs, who specialize in glass and pottery making. In the centre of the town stands the Haram (Sanctuary), built over the traditional site of the Machpelah cave. The rectangular structure is surrounded by a high wall, smooth below and pillared above, the work of King Herod. Inside a vaulted Crusader church has been turned into a mosque, in which stand the cenotaphs of the patriarchs and their wives, made of coloured marble. The burials themselves are supposed to be in the inaccessible caves below. A fine pulpit, brought by Saladin from Egypt, stands near the praying niche of the mosque.

Heptapegon (et Tabgha, in Arabic; Eyn ha-Shivah, in Hebrew) [DC]

Site on the shores of the Sea of Galilee north of Tiberias. Identified in Byzantine times as the location of the Miracle of the Loaves and the Fishes; a church was erected there in the 4th century and rebuilt in the 5th. The later church was paved with mosaics, two of which, in the transept, represent a Nilotic landscape, with birds, plants and buildings—including a Nilometer—which have been adjusted to the fauna and flora of the Genezareth shores. One of the finest mosaics in the Holy Land.

Herodium [GC]

National Monument. April to September 8–5; October to March 8–4.

Fortress of King Herod southeast of Bethlehem. Built in a circular shape on top of an artificial hill, it consisted of a double wall with three half-towers and a round tower on the east. Inside the fortress is a colonnaded portico and a thermal bath. The tomb of Herod, who was buried there according to Josephus, has not yet been found. The Zealots (or perhaps Herod himself) turned one of the inner rooms into a synagogue. The fortress served Bar Kokhba (132-135) as a command post and was later a Byzantine monastery.

Jaffa [FB]

Ancient port in central Palestine, now joined to Tel Aviv. Originally a Canaanite city mentioned in Egyptian sources from the 15th century BC onwards (Jaffa was taken by a ruse by the army of Thutmosis III of Egypt) and in the el-Amarna letters of the 14th century. It was the northernmost of the cities held by the Philistines. Solomon had the cedars brought to the sea of Jaffa from the Lebanon for the First Temple, and Jonah started on his ill-fated journey from there. The time of the occupation of Jaffa by the Egyptian dynasty of the 7th century BC, originally Ethiopians, gave the occasion for the localization there of the legend of Perseus and Andromeda, who was an Ethiopian princess. In Persian times Jaffa was held by the Sidonians; the Hasmonaeans occupied the port and made it their 'way to the isles of the sea' (*Macc. 14:5*). It remained a Jewish town till Byzantine times. It remained the main harbour for pilgrimages to Jerusalem in Crusader and later times, till overshadowed first by Haifa and then by Tel Aviv. The site of the ancient town is a mound overlooking the former harbour. Excavations there have produced the remains of Egyptian fortifications from the time of Rameses II, of Israelite and Hellenistic walls, and of the Roman town of Flavia Joppe. The single finds are kept at the Antiquities Museum. The Old City of Jaffa has been restored as an artists' quarter and tourist resort by the architects Frenkel, Mendel and Yaar.

Jericho [GC]

Ancient site in an oasis near the Jordan, close to the modern city of Jericho and to Elisha's Fountain (Ain el Sultan). Jericho is one of the oldest cities in the world: it had a wall and towers already in the

Neolithic period, in the 8th millennium BC. The site has been excavated by three expeditions, an Austrian one in 1907-9 and two English ones (1930-36 and 1952-58). It was found that the Early Bronze Age wall rested directly on the Neolithic remains. In the Middle Bronze Age the walls were rebuilt and a large buttressing glacis was added to them. No evidence of the walling of the Late Bronze period has been found, and it is assumed that the Canaanites of that period, who were conquered by Joshua after the famous incident of the walls which were miraculously blown down, were still using the earlier walls. The Neolithic tower is a huge structure with an inner staircase. A Herodian palace was found 2.5 km. west of the town and a Byzantine synagogue with a well preserved pavement was found near the Canaanite site. The pavement, which is aniconic, contains representations of the Ark of the Law and a seven-branched candlestick with the inscription 'Peace upon Israel'. Another inscription in six lines commemorates the building of the synagogue.

Jerusalem [GC]
Situated in the Judaean mountains slightly east of the watershed. Today Jerusalem consists of a walled-in Old City, containing most of the ancient monuments, and a modern city stretching out south, north and especially west.

THE OLD CITY
AND ITS VICINITY

Antonia Fortress. Remains of it, including a double cistern (the Struthion) and the pavement of the inner court (Lithostrotos) (*John 19:13*) are visible inside the Convent of Notre Dame de Sion, Via Dolorosa. The Antonia was built by Herod to protect the Temple on the north side. It is there that Pilate is supposed by many scholars to have judged Jesus.

El-Aqsa Mosque. The 'furthest' mosque mentioned in the Koran in sura 17 which describes Mohammed's night ride on his steed al-Buraq to heaven. The first Muslim prayer house in Jerusalem was erected on this site, which borders on the southern wall of the Temple esplanade. The oldest parts of the el-Aqsa now visible are Fatimid (façade, apse at the back and mosaics of the arch); the other parts are Crusader or modern, imitating the old building style. Below the Aqsa is the Double Gate of the Herodian age, with an underground tunnel.

Ascension, Church of the. Byzantine church with Crusader additions, on the Mount of Olives where Jesus's ascension to heaven is located by tradition (*Luke 24:51*). The church is octagonal, with an inside rotunda on columns, open to the sky.

David, Tomb of. Traditional site of the tomb of David (the actual site is on the Ophel hill, the real Mount Zion). The tomb, a very large Crusader sarcophagus, is covered up and the room is used for Jewish prayers. The back wall has an apse, possibly of a 4th-century synagogue. A *qibla* (praying niche) is placed in the south wall of the ante-room, for the site was used as a Muslim place of prayer. The Coenaculum is above this tomb.

Citadel (open 8.30–5). Adjoining Jaffa Gate, the Citadel stands on part of Herod's palace. Its northeastern tower has its Herodian base intact to a height of 20 m.—it was the base of Herod's tower Phasael. The other towers and the curtain wall are Crusader or Mameluke work. Inside are visible the foundations of the First Wall of Jerusalem from the Hasmonaean period, into which Phasael was set. Some of the foundations on which Herod's palace stood have also been excavated. A Roman sarcophagus with images of the Seasons stands in the octagonal entrance.

Coenaculum. Medieval vaulted hall over the Tomb of David on Mount Zion. Traditional site of the Last Supper.

Dome of the Rock (wrongly called the Mosque of Omar). Octagonal structure built over the rock jutting out in the centre of the Temple Mount. The outer walls are covered with marble slabs below and with Turkish faience tiles, the gift of Sultan Suleiman I, above. Inside there is an inner octagon with pillars covered with marble, and an inner circle of columns (re-used from Roman temples) carries the dome. The dome and the drum are covered with fine mosaics with floral ornaments and arabesques. Built in 691 by the Umayyad Caliph, Abd-el-Malik.

Ecce Homo arch. Central span of Roman arch over Via Dolorosa, near Convent of Notre Dame de Sion. The smaller side portal and part of the central span are visible inside the church of the Convent. Probably a triumphal arch built for Hadrian after the foundation of Aelia Capitolina.

Gates and Walls of the Old City. The present walls of the Old City follow the squarish outline of the Roman colony of Aelia Capitolina. The walls themselves stand partly on older foundations; in their present state they are the work of the Ottoman Sultan Suleiman I (inscription at Jaffa Gate and elsewhere). The gates of the Old City are at present seven.

Haram esh-Sherif - see *Temple Mount.*

Jaffa Gate, with the adjoining breach in the wall made for the solemn entrance of the German Kaiser Wilhelm II in 1898; the *New Gate* made by Sultan Abdul-Hamid II; *Damascus Gate,* the main northern gate, called in Arabic *Bab el-Amud,* 'Gate of the Pillar', in memory of a Roman pillar standing behind it and represented on the Madaba mosaic map. This gate is very ornate and of Mameluke workmanship. Below it are the excavated towers and part of a Roman gate, *Herod's Gate,* in Arabic *Bab ez-Zahira,* the quarter opposite; the *Lion's Gate* on the east (the only gate on that side, the Golden Gate being blocked) is ornamented on its façade by reliefs of lions, the armorial beast of the Mameluke sultan Baybars; the *Dung Gate* in the southern wall near the Wailing Wall, and the *Zion Gate* between the Armenian quarter and Mount Zion.

Gethsemane. Garden with olive trees east of the Old City, on the Mount of Olives. A Catholic church has been built on the foundations of a Byzantine and Crusader one; above it is a Russian church. It is the traditional site of Jesus's agony and arrest. (*Matthew 26:36*).

Holy Sepulchre, Church of the. Main Christian sanctuary of Jerusalem, built over remains of Constantine's basilica and rotunda. The façade and belfry are Crusader work; inside, the rotunda, with a dome, surrounds the aedicule within which a marble plaque covers the stone of the traditional tomb of Jesus. The adjoining ambulatory is also Crusader, with a 19th-century apse. Branching out from the ambulatory the Calvary chapel on a jutting rock identified as Golgotha, and the crypt of St Helena, where the True Cross is reported to have been found in 325.

Kidron Valley Tombs. Rock-cut tombs from the time of the Second Temple, on the eastern slope of the Kidron Valley. They include the 'Tomb of Absalom', the tomb of the priestly family of Bene Hezir (called the 'Tomb of St James') and the 'Tomb of Zechariah', which is one unit with the former.

Mary the Great. Crusader church near the Holy Sepulchre, over which the German *Erloeserkirche* has been built. Some architectural fragments of the Romanesque period are still visible.

Nea. The 'New' Church of the Virgin Mary built by Justinian opposite the Temple Mount, one of the greatest churches of Byzantine Jerusalem. The foundation of one of its apses was found in the Jewish quarter of the Old City in 1970.

Ophel. Name current among archaeologists for the City of David, a long and narrow hill outside the city wall between the Tyropoeon Valley and the Kidron Valley. The Gihon spring issues near its eastern slope and is carried by the Tunnel of the Pool of Siloam in the other valley. Remains of the wall of Jebusite Jerusalem, and of Israelite walls and houses are visible near the spring; higher up one can see a Hasmonaean tower and a bastion of the same date.

Russian Compound near the Holy Sepulchre (Alexandrovsky). Remains of the gate of the Roman forum and parts of the Constantinian basilica.

Sanhedriya Tombs (Tombs of the Judges). Group of rock-cut tombs with some ornamented façade in a park at the end of the Kidron Valley. The tombs date from the time of the Second Temple.

St Anne, Church of, and the *Sheep's Pool.* Crusader church near the traditional site of the Pool of Bezetha or Bethesda, also called Probatike or Sheep's Pool. The twin pools were separated by a dam, on which a Byzantine and Crusader church was built with the help of supporting arches. The present church is of pure Romanesque type; it was turned by Saladin into a mosque, but was restored to the Catholics by the intervention of Napoleon III.

St James. Armenian cathedral in the Armenian quarter of the Old City. Interior decorated with fine glazed tiles. The church is partly medieval and partly of the 18th century.

Solomon's Quarries (open 9–5). Extensive underground caverns, the so-called Royal Caverns of Josephus; popularly called the 'Cave of Zedekiah' the last king of Judah. They extend from Damascus Gate deep into the Old City in the direction of the Temple Mount.

Temple Mount or *Haram esh-Sherif* ('The Noble Sanctuary') (*visiting* hours 8–11, 1–5). Esplanade with supporting walls of the Herodian period. This open site takes up about one-sixth of the area of the Old City. On it stood the Second Temple (the First Solomonic Temple had smaller courts). Now the Dome of the Rock with its elevated platform occupies the centre, the Aqsa mosque stands on the southern side, and the whole is encircled by arched porticoes, and Muslim Madrasas and Zawiyas (schools of learning and monasteries). The area contains the fountain of Qaytbay and several others, various smaller domes, pulpits and praying areas. There are numerous cisterns underground, the largest of which, called el-Kas (the Goblet) is near the Aqsa mosque and serves the Muslim ablutions before prayer.

Tomb of Herod's Family. Tomb mentioned in Josephus, built by Herod for the members of his family. Now near the King David Hotel. It has a rolling stone and several underground chambers with walls covered by stone plaques.

Tomb of the Kings. Monumental funerary installation made for the kings of Adiabene (Helena and her children) in the 1st century AD. The family adopted Judaism and settled in Jerusalem. The tomb consists of a monumental rock-cut staircase, a rock-cut court, a portal with a Doric frieze and plant ornament in relief above it. The entrance to the burial cave is closed by a rolling stone. The architectural fragments found include parts of the three pyramids which surmounted the tomb.

Tomb of the Virgin Mary. In the Kidron Valley and the Dormitio on Mount Zion. The Mother of Jesus, according to tradition, 'fell asleep' in a house adjoining the Zion church. A modern church has beeen erected near the spot. Her tomb, with its Crusader façade, is shown in the Kidron Valley below the Lion's Gate, which is also called the Gate of the Lady Mary. *Upper City.* In the Jewish quarter. Excavations have revealed the remains of houses of the 8th and 7th centuries BC and a wall across the area dating to the time of Hezekiah. Later remains include parts of Hasmonaean and Herodian houses, down to the destruction wrought by Titus. One house still has traces of the conflagration of 70.

Via Dolorosa. The traditional route of Jesus carrying the Cross from the Antonia fortress to Golgotha. It begins near the Lion's Gate and passes westwards with two sharp

bends. The tradition dates from Crusader times; the present street level is several metres higher than in the time of Jesus.

Wailing Wall, or *Western Wall* (*open 8.30–11.30, 6.30–8*). Part of the western enclosure wall of the Herodian temple, where Jews have been wont to pray for many centuries. The area in front of the wall was greatly enlarged after 1967. North of the wall an arch of the old bridge crossing the Tyropoeon Valley ('Wilson's Arch') can be visited after passing many underground passages of medieval date.

MONUMENTS OUTSIDE THE OLD CITY

These include the Monastery of the Cross (11th century on Byzantine foundations), the traditional site of the tree from which the Cross was made. Beyond it is the representative area of modern Jerusalem: the Israel Museum, by Alfred Mansfeld and Dora Gad, including the Shrine of the Book by Kiesler and Bartos, and the Billy Rose Sculpture Garden by Isamu Noguchi; the Knesset (Parliament) by Klarwein with mosaics and tapestries by Marc Chagall; the Giveat Ram Campus of the Hebrew University with a synagogue by Rau and Reznik (the old Scopus Campus is now being rebuilt east of the city). Further west are Mount Herzl with the Tomb of Theodore Herzl, the founder of the Zionist Organization and the Yad va-Shem Memorial of the Holocaust by Arieh Elhanani; still further are the Hadassah Hospital in the synagogue of which are the stained glass windows by Chagall, and the Kennedy Memorial by Reznik. The tomb of Jason, on the Alfasi Road, is a tomb of the Hasmonaean period surmounted by a pyramid, excavated and reconstructed (visit by arrangement with the Department of Antiquities).

Jisr Jindas [GB]
Bridge between Lod and the Tel Aviv airport, built by the Mameluke sultan Baybars and marked with his lions in relief.

Kadesh (Cadasa) [DC]
Ruin near Hazor, with remains of a Roman temple of the sun, of the 2nd/3rd century.

Kefar Bar'am [DC]
National Monument. Summer 8–5; winter 8–4.
Ruined village near the Lebanese border, with the best preserved remains of all Galilean synagogues of

the early type (3rd century). The synagogue measures 20 x 15 m. Its façade, facing Jerusalem, has been preserved above the three portals, to the height of the relieving arch over the main gate and the windows over the side doors. Part of the portico is also still standing. The interior was plain and had benches along two of its walls. Three rows of columns (two lengthwise, one across) supported the roof; the columns stood on high pedestals. Over the central portal is sculptured a wreath supported by two flying figures which have been cut away by later iconoclasts.

Mampsis (Kurnub, Mamshit) [JB]
National Monument. Winter 8–4; Summer 8–5.
Nabataean-Byzantine site 40 km. southeast of Beersheba. The town existed between the 2nd and the 8th centuries AD. The remains are of a walled town, with several dams in a valley nearby. Inside the walls are remains of Nabataean houses re-used by the Byzantines, standing up to the second floor with winding staircases. Stables adjoin the houses. There is a caravanserai and a public bath, with a pool. Two Byzantine churches with mosaic pavements were erected over some of the Nabataean remains.

Mamre (Ramet el-Khalil, Beth Ilanim) [HB]
Traditional site of the Oaks of Mamre, 3 km. north of Hebron. Excavations in 1926-28 laid bare a Herodian enclosure with a well in its southwestern corner (the 'Well of Abraham' where pilgrims used to deposit their offerings). The stones of the Herodian wall (65 x 50 m.) are of a monumental type. In the time of Constantine a church was erected at the east end of the enclosure, consisting of a nave with inscribed apse, and two aisles with the prothesis and diakonicon adjoining the wall.

Mar Saba [GC]
Monastery in the Judaean desert, in the Kidron Valley. Founded by St Sabas (439-532), the great monastic leader of the Byzantine period, it is perched over the canyon, preserving almost unchanged the atmosphere of the early Christian hermitages.

Masada [HC]
Open 8–4. Jewish fortress standing on an isolated rock 300 m. high overlooking the western shores of the Dead Sea. It was selected as a stronghold by Alexander Jannaeus. Herod transformed the site about 30 BC. He built a casemate wall around the whole rock, which measures 600 x 300 m. Within this area he erected a palace with a throne room, residential quarters, work rooms and stores. Two additional dwelling houses and a bathing pool were provided near the palace. North of it were the barracks of the royal guard and the store houses with food and arms for 1,000 men; the stores had their own administrative building. Near them was a large public bath with hypocausts, built on the Roman system. The northern tip of the rock was cut off from the rest by a high wall with a single gate. Beyond it stood the private villa of the king in three tiers; on the upper terrace a small dwelling house with a round terrace in front of it; on the middle tier a round colonnaded tholos, the purpose of which is not yet clear; and on the lowest terrace an open court or hall, surrounded by a peristyle. Attached to it were another small bath and some dwelling rooms. The zealots who were in possession of Masada used the casemates as dwelling space and added two ritual baths; they also transformed the (Herodian?) synagogue by adding a small corner room. Around Masada can be seen the siege works with which the Romans took the rock. On the west is the siege dam, starting from a white rock (the Leuke); there are two large camps, each for half a legion, one in the plain below, the other in the west; six smaller camps are dotted along the line of the siege wall which entirely surrounds Masada, apart from some inaccessible cliffs on the south. On the northern slope of the fortress are underground cisterns in two tiers, once fed by aqueducts from the valleys in the Judaean hills.
Access to Masada is by 'Snake path' or cable car from the east, or by the siege dam from a road head in the west.

Mefjer, Khirbet [GC]
Winter palace of the Umayyad Caliph Hisham (724-43). Excavated 1932-39. The whole complex is entered by an ornamental gate, followed by a court with a fountain decorated with sculptures. The palace proper stands to the west; it consists of rooms around an open courtyard. The palace gateway is provided with benches and its walls are richly ornamented with stucco reliefs of arabesques and human heads. There is a private mosque with foundations of a square minaret on the south side, a throne room with an underground crypt for summer days below it on the west, and a dining hall on the north. The palace had an upper storey; the ornate central window

276

of this second floor has been reconstructed. Adjoining the palace was a public mosque and further north an extensive hall, once arched over with many domes on pillars. Its entire surface is paved with mosaics. Behind it is a public latrine and a small bath, the floor of which is adorned by a fine mosaic with the Tree of Life and a lion killing gazelles. The front, walls and roof of this hall were ornamented with stucco figures (now in the Rockefeller Museum) representing the Caliph, soldiers, dancers, beasts, birds. The site gives a curious sidelight on Umayyad culture at the Caliph's court.

Megiddo [EB]

National Monument, Winter 8–4; summer 8–5.
Canaanite and Israelite city, situated at the issue of the Megiddo pass connecting the coastal plain and the Valley of Jezreel. The earliest settlement was in the Chalcolithic period; the huge Canaanite mound began its existence in the Early Bronze period, from which two temples and a high place have been preserved. It was at Megiddo that Thutmosis III defeated the Hittites and Canaanites in a famous battle (1486 BC); the name Armageddon ("Mount Megiddo") in *Revelations 16:16* commemorates the great battles fought near this place. Here, in addition to the battles of Thutmosis, Josiah of Judah fought against Necho of Egypt in 609 BC and in 1917 Allenby fought against the Turks. Megiddo was taken by David and fortified by Solomon as one of his chariot cities. The casemate wall of Solomon, his gate and the foundations of his palace have been excavated and are visible. After Solomon, Ahab of Israel built a new wall and gates for Megiddo, erected huge stables for his chariot horses and dug the water tunnel with steps, securing the water supply of the fortress. The foundations of the house of his governor have also been preserved. The site was excavated in 1903-5, 1925-39 and 1968.

Meiron [DC]

Village 5 km. northwest of Safed in Upper Galilee. It contains the ruins of a synagogue of the 3rd century. The building measures 27 x 13.5 m.; its west side is cut in the rock. In the interior are three rows of columns, two lengthwise and one across. The synagogue had three portals in the façade to the south, facing Jerusalem (the third was reconstructed recently). The village contains also the traditional tomb of Rabbi Simeon Bar Yohai, the reputed father of the Cabbala. Every year a great

popular festivity is held on the spot on the 18th of Iyar (Lag be-Omer).

Minya, Khirbet (Horvat Minnim) [EC]

Palace of the Umayyad caliph Walid I (705-715) on the shores of the Sea of Galilee. Partly excavated in 1932, 1939 and 1959. The palace is a square structure with round towers in the corners. The gateway in the east is an ornate structure. The inside is planned as an open court with rooms along the walls; there was an upper storey with a ramp leading to it. A mosque stands in the southern part of the palace. The rooms adjoining it are paved with fine geometric mosaics.

Montfort (Qal'at el Qurein, Starkenburg) [DC]

Castle and headquarters of the Teutonic Order in Upper Galilee. 12 km. from the sea. The castle was sold to the order in 1220 and was held by it till 1271. It was excavated in 1926. The castle stands on a mountain spur; it was cut off by a deep fosse from the spur. The fosse is dominated by a high keep. The remains include an outer wall, the foundations of a chapel and refectory, deep cellars and an outer tower. The castle was not intended to dominate the countryside, but to provide a safe refuge for the archives and treasures of the order.

Nahariya [DB]

Town and seaside resort on the coast, north of Acre. A Middle Bronze (Canaanite) temple with adjoining high place has been excavated near the coast in 1947, 1954-55. It was dedicated probably to the Asherah of the Sea, a Phoenician goddess.

Nazareth [EC]

Town (formerly village) in Galilee, the place where Joseph and Mary lived, and where Jesus grew to manhood. In the 2nd century AD it was settled by a priestly family fleeing Jerusalem. The village remained Jewish into Byzantine times. The Byzantines built a church on the traditional site of the Annunciation, destroying in the process the rock-cut remains of earlier houses and cisterns. The Crusaders built a larger church over the remains of the Byzantine one; the capitals prepared for that church are kept in the Franciscan Museum and are among the finest examples of French 12th-century sculpture: they represent the martyrdom of St James and various miracles of Christ. The modern church of the Annunciation was built over the traditional "Cave of the Annunciation" with the granite

"Column of Gabriel". Nearby is the Church of St Joseph built on the traditional site of his workshop; a rock cave beneath the church is regarded as the home of Mary and Joseph. A spring by the road of Tiberias has been identified in Christian tradition with the well of Mary. Near it is the 18th-century Greek Orthodox Church of Gabriel, connected by that church with the Annunciation.

Nirim [HA]

Kibbutz in the southern coastal plain. On its land the ruin of a synagogue of Maon, a Jewish village in the region of Gaza was discovered in 1957-58. The synagogue measured 17 x 15 m. It was basilical in shape, with an apse pointing to Jerusalem and two rows of columns inside. Only the space between the columns was partly paved with mosaics. The pavement, probably executed by artists from Gaza, and dated to about 530, shows a vine trellis covering the whole surface, issuing from an amphora flanked by two peacocks. The trellis formed fifty medallions, in rows of five, with offerings represented in the middle row and symmetrical pairs of animals in the other medallions. At the apse end of the pavement is a seven-branched candlestick flanked by two lions and two palm trees, with Jewish ritual objects. The pavement is one of the finest examples of the later synagogue mosaics and is now exhibited in the Israel Museum.

Qumran, Khirbet (Mesad ha-Hasidim) [GC]

National Monument, Winter 8–4; summer 8–5.

Ruined monastery of the Dead Sea Sect, near the shore of the Dead Sea, south of Jericho. The site was excavated in 1951-56, after the discovery of the Dead Sea Scrolls, in one of the caves of a cliff across the valley. The sect settled there in the time of John Hycranus (135-104 BC), abandoned it for a short time in the time of Herod, returned in the time of Archelaus (4 BC-AD 6) and remained there till the Romans destroyed Qumran in 67/68. The ruins are composed of a square main building with a tower in its northwest corner, a scriptorium, assembly room and a kitchen. Around it were grouped various other buildings: a large dining hall for the common meals, stables, a potter's workshop among them. Water was brought from an aqueduct in the Judaean mountains to the west and collected in numerous stepped bathing pools, seven of which have been found.

The sect stressed purification by ablution in its ritual. One of the pools bears clear traces of an earthquake, probably that of 32 BC.

Ramat Rahel [GC]

Kibbutz 4 km. south of Jerusalem. Near it a Judaean palace and an administrative centre, as well as a Byzantine church, were excavated in 1960-62. The earliest buildings are dated to the 7th century BC; they include a casemate wall enclosing a rectangular court, with a gateway on the west and a palace on the east. The architectural details found include proto-Aeolic ("lotus") capitals and a balustrade for a window such as is represented on Israelite ivories. The building continued to be used after the return to Zion as an administrative centre, possibly the headquarters of the sub-district of Netopha. Later there were Herodian buildings, a Roman villa with works of the tenth legion, which garrisoned Jerusalem, and a Byzantine monastery. Near it was a basilical church, identified with the Kathisma church, so-called after the rest of the Virgin Mary on the way to Bethlehem.

Ramla [GB]

Town founded by Suleiman ibn Abd al Malik of the Umayyad dynasty at the beginning of the 8th century. It received its name from the sand (Arabic *raml*) on which it was built. The town lies on the Jerusalem-Tel Aviv highway. Its principal monuments are the Great Mosque, formerly the Crusader Cathedral of St John, and the White Mosque. The latter is a complex of buildings set within a large enclosure (93 x 84 m.). The mosque proper stands to the south. It is a long building with thirteen doors. It dates partly to the Umayyad and partly to the Ayyubid period. In the centre of the courtyards are two big cisterns. The minaret of the mosque is a conspicuous landmark built by the sultan Qalaun (1318) of the Mamelukes. Another monument at Ramla is the Uneiziyye cistern, completed in 789. It measures 24 x 20.5 m., the roof resting on three rows of piers with pointed arches, which form 24 cells, each with its own opening in the roof. This is the first example of a pointed arch in Muslim architecture.

Safed [DC]

City in Upper Galilee, first mentioned by Josephus in the 1st century AD as Sepph, and then in Talmudic literature. It was fortified by the Crusaders in the 12th century (Fulk of Anjou 1140; Templars in the reign of Amalric I 1168); taken by Saladin

(1188) and dismantled in 1220. Reoccupied by the Templars in 1240, captured by Baybars in 1266, Safed was the seat of the Mameluke viceroy of Galilee. In the 15th and 16th centuries there was a great influx of Spanish Jews, among them many Cabbalists, the most prominent of whom was Rabbi Isaac Lurie, known as ARI (1531-73). Two synagogues are connected with his name, a Sephardic and an Ashkenazi, one built during his lifetime, the other shortly after his death. The old cemetery at Safed includes the tombs of ARI, his master Cordoviero, and of Joseph Caro (died 1575), the author of the Shulkhan Arukh, the binding code of Orthodox Jewry. The Mameluke buildings at Safed include the Red Mosque (al-Jami' el-Ahmar) built by Baybars in 1275, and the tomb of the amir Muzaffar-ad-din Musa (1372). The town has an artists' colony in a picturesque quarter below the citadel.

Samaria-Sebaste [FB]
National Monument. Winter 8–4; summer 8–5.
Capital of the northern kingdom of Israel in biblical times, it was founded by Omri in 880 BC. It remained the residence of the kings of Israel till its capture by the Assyrians in 721 BC. Sargon II settled Cuthaeans there from Babylon, who, together with a remnant of the Israelites, formed the nucleus of the Samaritan community which took its name from this town. After a Samaritan revolt against Alexander, his successors settled in Samaria, a colony of Macedonian veterans. The city was taken by John Hyrcanus the Hasmonaean, and partly destroyed. It was rebuilt by Herod, who changed its name to Sebaste in honour of Augustus (*Sebastos* in Greek). Herod added two round gate towers to the existing wall with Hellenistic towers, and he provided the city with a temple of Augustus. Among later rulers Septimius Severus favoured Sebaste, making it into a Roman colony and providing its forum with a basilica. The worship of Kore was common in Sebaste; later on Christian tradition located there the finding of the head of St John the Baptist, and a Crusader church was erected in his honour.
The ruined site extends on a hill, dominating the surroundings, 12 km. northwest of Nablus, in the mountains of Ephraim. The visible remains include the forum with the Severan basilica, many columns of which are still standing; the Roman theatre with the Hellenistic tower near it;

the Herodian gate towers at the entrance to a colonnaded street. From there one can mount to the acropolis, where Israelite masonry (characterized by a boss in the centre and margins on three sides) can be seen. There stood the "house of ivory" of Ahab (*1 Kings 22:39*) from which many ivory fragments (now in the Rockefeller and Israel Museums) have been recovered. The staircase to the platform of the temple of Augustus still stands. Following the colonnaded street one passes the temple of Kore and an Israelite gateway near the forum. Samaria was excavated 1908-10 and 1931-35.

Shavey Zion [DB]
Village 8 km. north of Acre on the coast. A Byzantine church of the 5th century was excavated there in 1955 and 1957. In front of the church is a paved court, from which one ascends by a broad staircase to the outer narthex, the pavement of which is dated by an inscription to 486. The basilica proper has an inner narthex, a nave and two aisles; in the north aisle the symbol of the cross is visible within a circle; other crosses in the nave were under altar tables. The rooms adjoining the church on the northeast also had crosses on their pavements, but these were later covered by another mosaic design.

Shechem (Balata) [FC]
Canaanite and Israelite city, the precursor of modern Nablus. It is situated just outside the eastern entrance to that city. Owing to its position in a fertile and well-watered valley in the centre of the mountains of Ephraim, Shechem was one of the earliest and most powerful Canaanite cities, from the 2nd millennium onwards. The family of Jacob camped near by, and the relations with the Israelites remained friendly afterwards (in spite of the incident of Dinah, *Genesis 34*); when Joshua conquered Canaan Shechem apparently did not need to be taken. The first efforts at establishing a royalty in Israel (by Abimelech the son of Gideon, *Judges 9*) were connected with Shechem. The city remained a Samaritan centre, especially after the settlement of Samaria with Macedonians, till replaced about 71 by Neapolis (Nablus). The excavations at Shechem were carried out by Germans in 1913-14, 1926-27, and continued by an American team 1956-62. The remains visible are a monumental gate on the east and another on the north (with sections of a casemate wall); near the latter stood a large sanctuary within a

court walled off (a temenos). The sanctuary ("tower" migdal) was founded in the Middle Bronze Age. It measures 26 x 21 m. and has walls over 5 m. thick—thus making possible its use as a fortress. The towers flanked an entrance which was divided by a single column. Inside, the roof was supported by six columns in two rows.

Solomon's Pools [GB]

Group of three pools 5 km. south of Bethlehem, near the village of Urtas. The lowest pools is 177 m. long and 15 m. deep. There are four springs in the vicinity. The pools served the Jerusalem aqueducts in Roman times, and were frequently repaired till Mameluke times. The water supply from here to Jerusalem was renewed in 1919. The connection with Solomon rests on a verse in the *Song of Solomon 4:12* and is apocryphal. A Mameluke fortress built by Sultan Qalaun stands near the uppermost pool.

Subeita (Shivta, Isbeita [JA]

National Monument. Winter 8–4; summer 8–5.
Ruins of Byzantine town about 50 km. south of Beersheba, off the Nitzana road. The town was founded in Nabatean times, continued to exist under the Romans and flourished under the Byzantines. It was an open city, deriving its subsistence from the fields around it, which were irrigated by a sophisticated network of channels. Owing to its desert location most of the houses are still standing, some of them up to the second storey. The streets are narrow and winding. In the centre of the older portion of the town are public pools, which had to be cleared by the people as a civic obligation. Most of the houses had one or two private cisterns. Subeita has three churches: the southern one near the pools, with a baptistry adjoining its narthex. The church is tri-apsidal. A later mosque was so constructed as not to disturb the church. There is a central church and in the north a craftsmen's quarter with a third church, dedicated to St George, with atrium, narthex and baptistry. Subeita was excavated in 1934-38 and restored by the Parks authority.

Susiya, Khirbet [HB]

Ruined village 12 km. southeast of Hebron, on the Yatta road. Ruins of a synagogue of the Byzantine-Arab period are being excavated there. It consists of a court, a narthex and a broad room with a niche in the long north wall pointing to Jerusalem. The south wall still stands to its full height. The mosaic pavement has been damaged by iconoclasts and repaired; the original design had a Zodiac, Daniel in the Lion's Den, and an Ark of the Law flanked by two deer. (*Psalms 42:1*).

Tel Aviv [FB]

Coastal city, the largest city in Israel, founded in 1909 as a residential Jewish suburb of Jaffa. The haphazard construction by quarters and the lack of adequate road planning are still felt in the city, which is a centre of a conurbation of 600,000 people. Lacking in ancient monuments (apart from the ruined Tell Qasile north of the Yarkon river) Tel Aviv is the centre of modern culture in Israel—almost all the newspapers appear there, the theatres have a permanent housing in the city, and night life flourishes more than anywhere else. The city has the Mann Auditorium for concerts, by Carmi and Meltzer, the Habimah National Theatre, the Tel Aviv Museum by Yashar and Eytan, inaugurated in its new headquarters in 1971. Interesting houses from the 1920s and 1930s are in the centre of the town. Other interesting structures are the El-Al building by D. Carmi, the Hilton Hotel by Y. Rechter, and near Tel Aviv, the Bat-Yam Town Hall and the Dubiner House in Ramat-Gan, both by Hecker-Neumann-Sharon.

Tiberias [EC]

City on the western shore of the Sea of Galilee, founded by Herod Antipas, son of Herod, in AD 18 in honour of the emperor Tiberius. The city extended in Roman times south of the modern one, and joined Hammath Tiberias. Seat of the Jewish Patriarchate and Sanhedrin from the 3rd to the 7th centuries. A prosperous town under Arabs and Crusaders, ruined in Mameluke times. Attempts to revive it in the 16th century proved unavailing, and it was rebuilt only in the 18th by the Bedouin chief Dhahir el Omar who built its wall and citadel. Owing to its aura of sanctity many Jewish sages were buried here, including Maimonides (Moses son of Maimon); other tombs like Rabbi Akiva's are apocryphal.

Yehiam [DC]

National Monument. Winter 8–4; summer 8–5.
Crusader castle in Upper Galilee, 14 km. east of Nahariya. Originally the castle of Judin of the Templars, then the Teutonic knights; taken by Baybars in 1265, rebuilt by Dhahr el Omar as a palatial stronghold.

Painters, Sculptors and Architects

Adler, Yankel (1895-1949). Polish painter, having worked in Germany and England. Works in the Tel Aviv Museum, the Israel Museum and the Ein Harod Art Centre.

Agam, Yaakov (b. 1928). Israeli painter and sculptor resident in Paris. One of the pioneers of kinetic art. Various periods represented in the Israel Museum, the Tel Aviv Museum, and at the Convention Hall (Binyanei Haooma) of Jerusalem.

Alexandroni, Amnon (b. 1929). Israeli architect. Designed with A. Yaski residential area at Beersheba, and the Israel Petroleum Institute at Ramat Aviv 1967.

Alrod, Dan (b. 1934) and **Ilana** (b. 1936) Israeli architects. Designers of the Danish School in Jerusalem 1968.

Appel, Karel (b. 1921). Dutch painter. Works at the Israel Museum.

Archipenko, Alexander (1887-1964). Russian sculptor. Collection of painted cubist reliefs at the Tel Aviv Museum, sculpture in the Billy Rose Sculpture Garden at the Israel Museum.

Ardon, Mordecai (b. 1896). Israeli painter. Former pupil of Bauhaus. Several works of various periods in the Israel Museum.

Arikha, Avigdor (b. 1929). Israeli painter. Works in the Israel Museum, and a mosaic at the Soldier's Home in Jerusalem.

Aroch, Arieh (b. 1908). Israeli painter. Works of various periods in the Israel Museum.

Arp, Jean (1887-1966). French painter and sculptor. Monumental sculpture, *The Three Graces,* in King George Street, Jerusalem.

Attar, Haim (1902-53). Israeli painter. Founder of the Art Centre (Mishkan le 'Omanuth) of Ein Harod, where a collection of his works is featured.

Bacon, Francis (b. 1909). English painter. Portrait of Lucien Freud in the Israel Museum.

Bartos, Armand. American architect, designed the Shrine of the Book in the Israel Museum with F. Kiesler 1965.

Bourdelle, Antoine (1861-1929). French sculptor. Several works in the Billy Rose Sculpture Garden in the Israel Museum.

Braque, Georges (1882-1963). French painter and sculptor. Some paintings, one of which is of the Fauve period, and a sculpture in the Israel Museum.

Carmi, Dov (1905-62). Israeli architect. Designed the administrative building and the auditorium of the Hebrew University of Jerusalem, the Histadrut (Labour Federation) general quarters, the Mann Auditorium (with Meltzer), and the El Al building (with his son, Ram Carmi), all in Tel Aviv.

Cézanne, Paul (1839-1906). French painter. A landscape and two of his early paintings in the Israel Museum.

Chagall, Marc (b. 1887). Painter of Russian origin working in France. Several trips to Israel from 1932. Paintings of various periods in the Israel Museum and the Tel Aviv Museum. Stained glass windows in the Hadassah Medical Centre synagogue, tapestry and mosaics in the Knesset, Jerusalem.

Courbet, Gustave (1819-77). French painter. *The Wave* is in the Israel Museum.

Elhanani, Arieh (b. 1898). Israeli painter and architect. Designer of the Yad va-Shem Memorial in Jerusalem.

Ernst, Max (b. 1891). Painter from Brühl (near Cologne). Works in the Tel Aviv Museum.

Eytan, Dan (b. 1931). Israeli architect. Designed with Y. Yashar the new Tel Aviv Museum and the Mexican House at the Tel Aviv University.

Frenkel, Eliezer; Mendel, Seadia; Yaar, Yaacov. Group of Israeli architects, responsible for the reconstruction of old Jaffa.

Gauguin, Paul (1848-1903). French painter. A still life and two Tahiti canvases in the Israel Museum.

Gorky, Arshile (1904-48). American painter. Painting in the Israel Museum.

Gottlieb, Maurycy (1856-79). Polish Jewish painter. Paintings in the Tel Aviv Museum, the Israel Museum, and the Ein Harod Art Centre.

Hecker, Zvi (b. 1933). Israeli architect. Designed the Town Hall in Bat-Yam and the Dubiner House in Ramat–Gan with Alfred Neumann and Eldad Sharon, and the Mechanical Engineering Building at the Haifa Technion with Alfred Neumann.

Israels, Jozef (1824-1911). Dutch realist painter. Paintings in the Tel Aviv Museum, the Israel Museum and the Ein Harod Art Centre.

Janco, Marcel (b. 1895). Israeli painter. Co-founder of the Dada Movement in Zurich *c.* 1917, of the New Horizon Group 1948, and of the artists' village in Ein Harod. Works, especially of the Dada period, in the Tel Aviv Museum.

Karavan, Dany (b. 1930). Israeli sculptor. Designed the Stone Wall at the Knesset in Jerusalem, and a monument near Beersheba.

Kaufmann, Richard (1877-1958). Israeli architect. Designed the circular Nahalal moshav.

Kiesler, Frederick (1896-1966). Austrian/American architect. Designed the Shrine of the Book in the Israel Museum with A. Bartos.

Kisling, Moïse (1891-1953). Painter born in Cracow. Works of various periods in the Israel Museum, the Tel Aviv Museum and the Ein Harod Art Centre.

Klarwein, Joseph (1893-1970). Israeli architect. Designed the Knesset (Parliament) in Jerusalem.

Kokoschka, Oskar (b. 1886). Painter born in Austria. Travelled to Palestine in 1920 and about 1929-30. Works in the Israel Museum.

De Kooning, Willem (b. 1904). Dutch painter working in New York. Painting in the Israel Museum.

Krakauer, Leopold (1890-1954). Israeli architect and designer. Designed the dining rooms of the Beth Alpha and Tel-Yosef kibbutzim.

Lear, Edward (1796-1864). English painter. Travelled to Palestine in 1856 and 1869. Views of Jerusalem and Bethlehem in the Israel Museum.

Liebermann, Max (1847-1935). German painter. Several works in the Tel Aviv Museum, the Israel Museum and the Ein Harod Art Centre.

Lipchitz, Jacques (b. 1891). Russian-American sculptor having worked in Paris. Monumental works in the Israel Museum (Billy Rose Sculpture Garden) and in the Tel Aviv Museum. Collection of 130 bronzes at the Jacques Lipchitz Pavilion in the Israel Museum.

Louis, Morris (1912-62). American painter. Works in the Israel Museum at Jerusalem and the Tel Aviv Museum.

Maillol, Aristide (1861-1944). French sculptor. Several works in the Billy Rose Sculpture Garden in the Israel Museum.

Mansfeld, Alfred (b. 1912). Israeli architect. Designed the Israel Museum with Dora Gad.

Melnikov, Aharon (b. 1903). Israeli sculptor, creator of the *Lion* of Tel Hai.

Mendelssohn, Erich (1887-1953). German architect. Worked in Palestine 1934-41. Designed the Hadassah Medical Centre at Mount Scopus in Jerusalem, the Leumi Bank and the Schocken Library.

Moore, Henry (b. 1898). English sculptor. Works in the Billy Rose Sculpture Garden of the Israel Museum, in the Tel Aviv Museum and the Hebrew University of Jerusalem.

Neumann, Alfred (1900-69). Israeli architect. Designed the Town Hall at Bat-Yam and the Dubiner House in Ramat–Gan with Z. Hecker and E. Sharon, and, with Hecker, the Mechanical Engineering Building at the Haifa Technion.

Niemeyer, Oscar (b. 1907). Brazilian architect. Designer of Haifa University (in construction).

Noguchi, Isamu (b. 1904). American sculptor and landscape architect. Created the Billy Rose Sculpture Garden at the Israel Museum.

Palombo, David (1920-66). Israeli sculptor. Doors of the Yad va-Shem Memorial and of the Knesset in Jerusalem.

Pascin, Jules (1885-1930). Painter born in Bulgaria. Important collection of paintings, watercolours and drawing at the Israel Museum.

Picasso, Pablo (b. 1881). Spanish painter and sculptor. *Profile of a Woman* in the Billy Rose Sculpture Garden, paintings and an important collection of prints in the Israel Museum.

Pollock, Jackson (1912-56). American painter. Paintings in the Tel Aviv Museum.

Rau, Heinz (1896-1965). Israeli architect. Several apartment blocks and public buildings in Jerusalem. Designed the synagogue of the Hebrew University with David Reznik.

Rechter, Yaakov (b. 1924). Israeli architect. Designed the Tel Aviv Hilton 1965 and the Resort Hotel in Zichron Yaacov 1968.

Rewich, Erhard (active second half 15th century). Dutch painter and engraver. In 1483 he travelled in the Holy Land with Breydenbach and as a result illustrated with engravings the work *Peregrinationes in Terram Sanctum* (Mayence 1486).

Reznik, David (b. 1923). Israeli architect. Designed the synagogue of the Hebrew University of Jerusalem with Rau. Also in Jerusalem, the Kennedy Memorial, the Humanitarian Academy and the Soldier's Home, and in Ayyelet ha-Shahar, the Hazor Museum.

Roberts, David (1796-1864). English painter. Travelled to Palestine in 1829. One watercolour, *The Sepulchre Saint,* and his complete collection of lithographs in the Israel Museum.

Rodin, Auguste (1840-1917). French sculptor. *Adam* and the small *Balzac* in the Billy Rose Sculpture Garden in the Israel Museum.

Schatz, Boris (1867-1932). Israeli painter and sculptor, founder of the first art school in Jerusalem. Works in the Israel Museum.

Schiele, Egon (1890-1918). Austrian painter. Works in the Israel Museum and the Tel Aviv Museum.

Scorel, Jan van (1495-1562). Dutch painter. View of Jerusalem in the Utrecht Museum in the Netherlands.

Sebba, Shalom (b. 1897). Israeli painter and sculptor. Wall in the Ashkelon Civic Centre and paintings in the Tel Aviv Museum.

Sharon, Arieh (b. 1900). Israeli architect. Former pupil of Bauhaus. Designed the workers' flats in Tel Aviv and numerous public buildings.

Sharon, Eldad (b. 1934). Israeli architect. Responsible for the Town Hall in Bat-Yam and the Dubiner House in Ramat–Gan with Neumann and Hecker.

Sisley, Alfred (1839-99). French painter. *Landscape* in the Israel Museum.

Soutine, Chaim (1894-1943). Painter born in Smilovitch. *Landscapes* of the 1920s in the Tel Aviv and Israel Museums.

Tinguely, Jean (b. 1925). Swiss sculptor. Kinetic work in the Israel Museum.

Tumarkin, Yigael (b. 1933). Israeli painter and sculptor. Paintings and sculptures in the Israel and Tel Aviv Museums. Monumental works at Ashdod, Dimona and Arad (*Observation Post*).

Utrillo, Maurice (1883-1955). French painter. Paintings of various periods in the Tel Aviv and Israel Museums.

Van Gogh, Vincent (1853-90). Dutch painter. Two landscapes of 1888 in the Israel Museum.

Vasarély, Victor (b. 1908). Painter and sculptor born in Pecs, Hungary. Works in the Israel Museum, of which *The Screen* is in the Billy Rose Sculpture Garden.

Vlaminck, Maurice de (1876-1958). French painter. Paintings of various periods in the Tel Aviv and Israel Museums.

Yashar, Isaac (b. 1924). Israeli architect. Designed the new Tel Aviv Museum and the Mexican House at the Tel Aviv University with Eytan.

Yaski, Abraham (b. 1927). Israeli architect. Designed with Alexandroni a residential quarter in Beersheba and the Israel Petroleum Institute at Ramat Aviv 19667.

Zaritzky, Yosef (b. 1891). Israeli painter. Co-founder of the New Horizon Group in 1948. Works in the Israel and Tel Aviv Museums.

Acknowledgments

The Publishers wish to express their gratitude to the following for their assistance during the preparation of this book; The Department of Antiquities and Museums in the Ministry of Education, Jerusalem; The Directors of the Israel Museum Jerusalem, the Haaretz Museum, Tel Aviv; The Rockefeller Museum, Jerusalem; The Director of the Waqf, Jerusalem (for permission to photograph in the Dome of the Rock); Mr Mordechai Avida, Mrs Irene Levitt, Mrs Inna Pomeranz, Jerusalem and Miss Gusti Lederer, Tel Aviv.

Index

Glossary

Amazonomachy decoration depicting battle of the Amazons

Amphictyonic league of neighbouring states working for common interest

Aniconic of idols and symbols not shaped in human or animal form

Antinomism doctrine that moral law is not binding on Christians

Ashlar square hewn stones

Caduceus wand carried by messenger god, Hermes or Mercury

Casemate vaulted chamber in thickness of wall with embrasures

Counterscarp outer wall or slope of ditch supporting covered way

Cyma ogee moulding of cornice

Decumanus main gate of camp where tenth cohort was quartered

Glacis bank sloping down from fort on which attackers are exposed to fire

Haematite red, brown or blackish iron ore

Hepatoscopy divination by means of inspection of the liver

Hypocaust chamber with pipes by which heat from furnace was distributed through building

Mangonel military engine for casting stones

Nefesh monument above tomb chamber

Orthostat uprights of stone passage in megalithic cave dwelling

proto-Aeolic derived from Aeolia, a district of Asia Minor, applied to 'lotus' capitals

Sanhedrin highest court of justice in ancient Jerusalem

Satrap holder of provisional governorship in ancient Persian empire

Terre pisée combination of clay, gravel and straw used in building walls

Temenos sacred enclosure

Triglyph grooved tablet alternating with metope in Doric frieze

Voussoir wedge-shaped stones forming arch